THE MOUNTAIN BIKE GUIDE TO

THE VALLEYS OF SOUTH WALES THE GOWER PENINSULA & LOWER WYE VALLEY

21 ALL TERRAIN RIDES COMPILED AND PHOTOGRAPHED BY NICK COTTON

ISBN 871890 19 5

PUBLISHED BY CORDEE

CONTENTS

Contents

Introduction

Table of routes

Other routes in brief

Ride 1 *Coastline and hills on the Gower Peninsula*

Ride 2 *The Great Forestry Ride between Neath and Pontypridd*

Ride 3 *The rough Roman Road of Sarn Helen, above the Vale of Neath*

Ride 4 *Sarn Helen and the Neath Canal to the northeast of Neath*

Ride 5 *Afan Argoed and the Pontrhydyfen viaducts*

Ride 6 *Afan Argoed's network of easy trails*

Ride 7 *Margam Forest and the Cwm Dyffryn Railway Path*

Ride 8 *A moorland and forestry challenge north of Blaengarw*

Ride 9 *Ogmore Vale, Ogmore Forest and Mynydd William Meyrick*

Ride 10 *A double loop north of Brynna, between the Rhondda and Ogmore valleys*

Ride 11 *Into the forestry above Aberdare, between the Cynon and Taff valleys*

Ride 12 *Cwm Darran Country Park and the old mining village of New Tredegar*

Ride 13 *The Cefn Manmoel Ridge Ride to the west of Ebbw Vale*

Ride 14 *Coity Mountain between Abersychan and Abertillery*

Ride 15 *The Taff Trail between Cardiff and Merthyr Tydfil*

Ride 16 *Into the hills east of Castell Coch*

Ride 17 *Sirhowy Valley Country Park and the Rhymney Valley Ridgeway*

Ride 18 *Easy riding on the two canals north of Newport*

Ride 19 *Into the wooded hills of Wentwood Forest south of Usk*

Ride 20 *Two loops in the Wye Valley between Redbrook and Tintern*

Ride 21 *The Wye Valley from Wyesham, south of Monmouth*

Fold out Map of all 21 Rides

Ride Planning *Distances and Grades*

From the dazzling sweep of the white sandy beaches of the Gower to the glory of the changing autumn colours in the Wye Valley, from the network of canal towpaths, dismantled railways and forestry tracks to the unspoilt ridges between the old mining valleys, South Wales offers a huge variety of all terrain mountain bike rides to suit every ability. As the area comes to terms with the demise of the coal industry, opportunities are opening up for the development of a comprehensive network of tracks and trails linking valley with forest and town with countryside. The Taff Trail from Cardiff to Merthyr Tydfil shows what can be done if there is sufficient willpower.

With its links to the motorway network South Wales lies within three hours of over half the population of Britain: London, Birmingham, Manchester and most of the population between can easily access the delights of the Wye Valley, the coastal grandeur of the Gower, the vast swathes of Forestry Commisson land and the unexpected beauty of the ridges between the old coal mining valleys.

The area covered by this book divides naturally into one main area and two secondary ones. The main area is the heartland of South Wales collectively known as 'The Valleys'. The two secondary areas are the lower Wye Valley, between Monmouth and Chepstow, which features two rides and the Gower Peninsula to the west of Swansea which has just one ride.

THE WELSH VALLEYS

In its heyday during the Industrial Revolution the night skies glowed bright over Merthyr Tydfil as the round the clock blast furnaces smelted metal which was used to build railway lines in places as far afield as Siberia. Coal and iron were exported from South Wales all over the world but now the pits have been closed down and most of the steelworks have moved to the coast.

The pit heads and winding gear may have disappeared, the slag heaps may have been greened over but one is still aware of the industrial past in the form of densely packed terraced housing in every valley. Despite this the area has huge tracts of unspoilt upland, ideal for mountain biking: almost all the development is restricted to narrow ribbons along the valley floors. There are several collieries that have been turned into museums and should a sudden change of weather wreck your mountain biking plans you could do worse than visit one of the following:

Rhondda Heritage Park, Trehafod, to the west of Pontypridd on the A470 towards Porth. Tel: 01443 682036

Big Pit, Blaenavon Tel: 01495 792615

Cefn Coed Colliery Museum, 5 miles north of Neath on the A4109. Tel: 01639 750556.

Two novels give an indication of the conditions prevalent in the 19th century mining industry: *Rape of the Fair Country* by Alexander Cordell **and How Green Was My Valley** by Richard Llewelyn.

ACCOMMODATION

The best way to find appropriate accommodation whether you are looking for a campsite or a five star hotel is to ring the Tourist Information Centre close to where you wish to stay. If you call in at the TIC in person they will book the accommodation for you. The numbers of the relevant Tourist Information Centres are shown opposite.

The tourist infrastructure of the Valleys area is still in its infancy and in many ways, if you are planning to spend a weekend or longer exploring the area, it would be better to be based around Abergavenny and the Usk Valley and using the A465 Heads of the Valleys Road to access the rides in the eastern and central valleys. Villages along the Glamorgan Coast, particularly Ogmore-by-Sea, offer bases for exploring the western valleys. The Gower and Wye Valley have abundant choice of accommodation.

With its good network of fast roads (M4, A40, A449, A470 and A465) little more than an hour's drive lies between even the furthest apart of the rides. As for the rail network, in addition to the main Newport-Cardiff-Swansea line, there are connexions up the valleys from Newport to Abergavenny, and from Cardiff to Rhymney, Merthyr Tydfil, Aberdare and the Rhondda.

TOURIST INFORMATION CENTRES

Abergavenny Tel: 01873 857588
Brecon Tel: 01874 622485
Caerphilly Tel: 01222 880011
Cardiff Tel: 01222 227281
Chepstow Tel: 01291 623772
Crickhowell Tel: 01873 812105
Cwmcarn Tel: 01495 272001
Llanelli Tel: 01554 772020
Merthyr Tydfil Tel: 01685 379884
Monmouth Tel: 01600 713899
Mumbles Tel: 01792 361302
Newport Tel: 01633 842962
Pontneddfechan Tel: 01639 721795
Pontypridd Tel: 01443 409512
Swansea Tel: 01792 468321

It would be a brave man indeed who could put his hand on his heart and claim to have written a comprehensive guide to offroad biking in South Wales. There are so many tracks that fall into categories not covered by bridleway, byway or Road Used as Public Path (RUPP), so many Forestry Commission holdings with their hundreds of miles of tracks and so much ongoing development of old canal towpaths and disused railway lines that any guide must acknowledge that it cannot ever be complete and final. I have, nevertheless, tried to include as wide a selection of routes in the main part of the book as possible. In this section, Other Routes in Brief, a few more ideas are suggested that need to be studied in conjunction with the appropriate Ordnance Survey Landranger map.

FORESTRY *(from west to east, see map)*
Other than those areas described in the main section there are the following Forestry Commission holdings which offer year-round riding on good tracks:

*1. The huge swathes of forestry between the Tawe and the Taff valleys contain many hundreds of miles of tracks. Many of the areas are explored in the main section but that still leaves myriad options. Good bases are the Afan Argoed Country Park and Glyncorrwg, to the east of Neath, off the A4107 or Llanwonno, a tiny hamlet 5 miles northwest of Pontypridd. With a little application, using some sections of minor lanes and bridleways it would be posible to link all the various holdings (**OS Landranger** 170, **Explorer** 152, **Explorer** 166).*

*2. Cwmcarn, off the A467 between Newport and Newbridge near to Abercarn. There is also a Forest Drive here so you may occasionally come across cars in the woodland. (**OS Landranger** 171).*

*3. Wentwood Forest (5 miles northeast of Newport, **OS Landranger** 171). Ride 19 uses some tracks in Wentwood Forest.*

*4. Forest of Dean (**OS Landranger** 162, **Outdoor Leisure** 14).*

LANE NETWORKS
There may be times in the middle of winter when you want to go for a ride and cannot face the prospect of slow muddy tracks and would prefer to go for a blast on quiet lanes, knowing that you can cover a good distance without worrying about the surface you are riding on, without gates to open and happy that you can go into a pub in a reasonably presentable state. There are two areas which immediately spring to mind:

*1. The countryside lying to the south of the M4 between Cardiff and Bridgend has very few offroad tracks but a good network of lanes based around the market town of Cowbridge (**OS Landranger maps** 170, 171)*

*2. The square formed by Abergavenny, Monmouth, Chepstow and Newport has, with the exception of Wentwood Forest and the lower Wye Valley, relatively few bridleways and rideable tracks. As compensation there are hundreds of miles of excellent, quiet lanes linking many attractive villages and the handsome towns of Monmouth and Usk (**OS Landranger maps** 161, 162, 171).*

OTHER ROUTES IN BRIEF

TO THE WEST

(Pembrokeshire and the coast)
Draw a line north from Swansea to Aberystwyth and you cut off the whole of the 'prong' of West Wales. Within this area there are remarkably few offroad options: with the exception of Brechfa Forest, to the northeast of Camarthen and a few tracks over the Preseli Hills, the area is almost devoid of good offroad tracks. The lane network, however, is excellent and the coastal walking around the Pembrokeshire peninsula is some of the best in Britain.

TO THE NORTH

Mountain Bike Guide to the Brecon Beacons National Park and the Black Mountains, *(published by Cordee), describes* 20 all terrain rides in and around the Brecon Beacons National Park, which lies just to the north of the area covered by this book.

TO THE EAST

With the exceptions of the Monmouth-Chepstow section of the Wye Valley and the Forest of Dean there is little mountain biking between the Rivers Usk and Severn.

EASY CYCLING AND WAY MARKED FORESTRY RIDES

(Suitable for family/novices)

1. Newport–Cross Keys Canal.

2. Newport–Pontypool Canal.

3. Sirhowy Valley Country Park, west of Risca on A4048 (railway path/forestry).

4. Taff Trail (best bits lie north from the centre of Cardiff and north from Cefn Coed/Merthyr Tydfil to Brecon).

5. Afan Argoed Country Park, A4107 northeast of Port Talbot (railway path /forestry).

6. Ogmore Vale, A4061 north of Bridgend (railway path).

7. Neath Canal (southwest from Glyn Neath for 4 miles).

8. Wye Valley railway path south of Redbrook (A466, south of Monmouth).

9. South side of the River Wye near Biblins Bridge, south of Symonds Yat.

10. Abergavenny–Llanfoist Railway Path.

11. Abersychan–Pontypool Railway path.

12. Cwm Darran Country Park, northwest of the A469 through Bargoed.

13. The ridge track over Cefn Manmoel between the Sirhowy Valley and Ebbw Vale (north of the village of Manmoel GR 180035)

14. Garwnant Forestry Visitor Centre, on the A470 to the north of Merthyr Tydfil.

15. Swansea Bike Paths along the sea front from The Mumbles to the Marina and inland through Clyne Valley Country Park to Gowerton.

1

COASTLINE AND HILLS ON THE GOWER PENINSULA

DISTANCE
24 miles (39 kms)

TIME
4½ hours

GRADE
Strenuous

TERRAIN
Coastline and coastal views
from heather-clad hills

HILLS AND HIGHPOINTS
1st climb ▲ 610 ft (186 mts)
from Oxwich to the top of Cefn Bryn
2nd climb ▲ 460 ft (140 mts)
from Cheriton up onto Llanmadoc Hill
3rd climb ▲ 600 ft (183 mts)
from Hill End to the Beacon on Rhossili Down
Highest points ▲ 610 ft (186 mts)
at the top of Cefn Bryn near the start
▲ 640 ft (193 mts)
above Rhossili Bay
Total ascent ▲ 2680 ft (815 mts)

START
Oxwich car park, on the coast 10 miles
southwest of Swansea, to the south of the
A4118 (GR 501865)

PARKING
As above (£2 charge)

NEAREST RAILWAY
Gowerton, 8 miles northeast of the
route at Penmaen

REFRESHMENTS
Cafes in Oxwich and Rhossili
Britannia Inn, Cheriton
Kings Head PH, Llangennith
Countryman PH, Scurlage

YR YMDDIRIEDOLAETH GENEDLAETHOL · THE NATIONAL TRUST

BAE RHOSILI BAY

The Gower Peninsula
offers not only a superb ride
with two magnificent ridges
but also the chance of a swim
on two of the finest sandy
beaches in West Wales.
Oxwich at the start/end of the
ride and the vast sweep of
Rhossili Bay halfway round the
route. It is worth leaving this
ride for a fine day with good
visibility as the views both of
the Gower and right across to
Exmoor are truly spectacular.

The first part of the ride is the least pleasant: 3 miles on road with a steep climb up from Oxwich then a busy section along the A4118 into Penmaen. You will get this out of your way while you are fresh and soon tuck into the real feast, starting with the ridge route across Cefn Bryn. This offers fine views in all directions as you descend gently then more steeply over 4 miles along a wide, well-drained grassy track. All this and heaven too. Two short climbs either side of Burry Pill bring you to the pub in Cheriton and the second of the main climbs along the flanks of Llanmadoc Hill. This is as nothing compared to the highly strenuous push to get you on top of Rhossili Down. Below is the long sweeping arc of Rhossili Bay, the crumpled grass covered sand dunes and the curious rocky outcrops of Worms Head.

A tricky steep grassy descent leads on to the final third of the ride which is much more agricultural in feel. The peculiar road detour near the end of the ride from Hangman's Cross, avoiding what would appear to be a perfectly good bridleway, spares you the frustration of walking your bike down a deep, washed-out gully filled with loose stones. You have been warned!

1 Exit the car park at Oxwich and **turn R** towards main road (A4118). Flat section then steep climb. At T-junction with A4118 **turn R** 'Swansea'.

2 Follow this busy road for almost 2 miles, passing church and X-roads in Nicholaston, then 1/2 mile after 'Penmaen' sign at start of village **turn L** uphill on road by telephone box and bus shelter.

3 Climb for 600 yards then opposite house on the right with double metal gates **turn L** steeply uphill onto track. At T-junction of tracks **turn L, then immediately fork L** on the steeper of the two tracks. Climb past stone pumping station of Welsh Water on top of the hill. Fine views open up. Short descent then take **left hand fork** on the hill ahead. Maintain height.

4 At T-junction with road **go SA and diagonally L** onto track, shortly **forking R**

towards trig point. You will eventually go round the right hand end of the hills that you see ahead, although initially your course is towards the middle of the hills.

At the trig point **fork L**. Continue on the main track. 400 yards after passing beneath power lines carried by telegraph poles, as the descent steepens, **bear R** at fork towards the right hand edge of the hills.

5 At T-junction with broad stone track (GR 473910) **bear L**. Track turns to tarmac. At X-roads (white lines across road) **turn R** 'Fairy Hill'. At T-junction **turn L** 'Llangennith' then after 150 yards uphill **1st track R** 'Bridleway'.

6 Follow stone track to its end. At farmhouse **go SA** onto grassy track. Enter woodland and **bear R** steeply downhill on stone track. Cross stream and climb steeply. At T-junction with gravel track by barn conversion **turn L**. At T-junction with road **turn L**.

7 At T-junction by Britannia Inn **turn L** 'Llangenith'. Climb steeply for 1/2 mile. **Ignore** a 'Bridleway' sign pointing up the grassy slope to the right. Shortly after the second house on the left (called 'Hillcrest'), **turn sharp R** steeply uphill on broad gravel track.

8 Follow the stone track to its end by the second house and go **SA** onto enclosed, grassy track. At a ruined house **turn L** downhill on grass track, taking the **right hand fork** to join better stone track. At T-junction with road **turn R**. Go past pub and church in Llangennith. At small roundabout at the end of the village **turn L**.

9 Immediately before the entrance to the caravan site **turn L** through bridlegate 'NT Rhossili Down'. **You have a choice. Fork R** for low level route beneath the hillside with fine sea views or **fork L** for very steep push to the top of hill with magnificent views of all the Gower, a ridge ride then very steep grassy descent.

10 The two options merge. At T-junction with road **turn L** (or **turn R** for cafes in

Rhossili). After ½ mile take the **1st road L**
by bus shelter and telephone box onto
'No through road'.

11 At the end of tarmac **fork R**. After
¾ mile go through gate and follow track
round right hand bend ('Private' sign on track
ahead). Shortly, **fork R** onto stone track. Go
past ruin, along right hand edge of first field,
left hand edge of second field then through
gate onto enclosed track. At exit from enclosed
track **bear L** diagonally across field and
through gate onto second enclosed section.

12 Go past farm. After 400 yards, as
the main track swings sharp left, immediately
before the gate ahead **turn R** off the
main track through the other gate onto grassy
track. Go through second farm, passing a
church to your left. At T-junction with road
turn R. At T-junction with A4118 **turn R**
'Port Eynon'.

13 After 1 mile **1st road L** 'Berry'.
At T-junction by farm **turn R**. Tarmac turns to
track which narrows then swings right by
ruined house. At T-junction with road **turn L**
for ¾ mile then **1st road R** by triangle of
grass 'Oxwich' (**do not** be tempted by the
bridleway ahead unless you fancy pushing your
bike down a steep, badly eroded gully with
lots of loose rock!).

14 Follow road round left hand hairpin bend
'Oxwich'. At X-roads **turn L then R** to return
to the car park at the start.

2

THE GREAT FORESTRY RIDE BETWEEN NEATH AND PONTYPRIDD

DISTANCE
*30 miles (48 kms) one way
between the two railway stations
60 miles (96 kms) round trip*

TIME
4¹/₂ hours one way, 9 hours return

GRADE
*Strenuous. This is a very long ride but on
excellent quality surfaces so you can travel
faster than on the rougher surfaces
of most of the other rides*

TERRAIN
*Almost all forestry with some moorland.
Fine views down into the Vale of Neath
and Rhondda*

HILLS AND HIGHPOINTS
Neath to Pontypridd (west to east)
*One major climb ▲ 1870 ft (570 mts)
over 13 miles, from Neath to the highpoint
Two short climbs in the second half of the ride
▲ 230 ft (70 mts) and 295 ft (90 mts)*

Pontypridd to Neath (east to west)
*First major climb ▲ 1345 ft (410 mts)
from Pontypridd to the west of Llanwonno
Second major climb ▲ 820 ft (250 mts)
from the Rhondda Fach River valley to the
highpoint of the ride*

*Highpoint ▲ 1935 ft (590 mts)
on Mynydd Beili-glas just to the west
of the A4061
Total ascent ▲ 2790 ft (850 mts)
in each direction*

**As a there-and-back ride
this is the longest in the book,
30 miles each way between
Neath and Pontypridd,
although as it is linear it can
be as short or as long as you
choose. However as the ride
uses forestry tracks and minor
roads for its full course, plus
short sections of busier roads in
the town centres, it should be
possible for the very fit to go
there and back in a day.**

START

Neath or Pontypridd Railway Station, or see Parking below for alternative starting points away from the town centres

PARKING

1. At Neath or Pontypridd railway stations or if you wish to cut out the towns
2. At the picnic site in Mosshouse Wood near to Neath (GR774981)
3. At the church/pub in Llanwonno near to Pontypridd (GR030957)

NEAREST RAILWAY

The ride starts and finishes from railway stations at Neath and Pontypridd. There is a short cut option near to the highest point of the ride of descending on the A4061 to Treherbert and catching the train to Pontypridd

REFRESHMENTS

Not a lot apart from the start and finish! There is a pub en route in Llanwonno, 5 miles northwest of Pontypridd. Otherwise it will be necessary to lose a lot of height for supplies in Maerdy, Treherbert or Glyncorrwg

Improbable though it may seem, this long ride weaves its way through the densely populated region of South Wales involving little contact with built-up areas or industry. After leaving the last residential house on the outskirts of the two towns, the only real intrusions into the woods and moorlands that constitute the ride are the crossings of the two main roads (the A4061 and the A4233) and the views down to Maerdy in Rhondda Fach.
This is a ride that improves on each outing as you are able to cover big distances without looking at the map or the instructions. It could also be used as part of a training programme to build up big reserves of stamina. It would be easy to come up with any amount of circuits for the western half of the ride, returning from the highpoint via Glyncorrwg or Blaengwynfi and down the Afan valley as far as Pontrhydyfen and Efail Fach before the last few miles on the B4287 back to Neath. Think of the ride described below as a coathanger on which to hang your favourite options!

Another option is to make the highpoint of the ride (GR 907032) on Mynydd Beiliglas, at close to 2000 ft above sea level, so whether you start fromPontypridd or Neath you are faced with a largely downhill run for the second half of the ride.

Neath to Pontypridd (west to east)

1 *(If by any chance the one way system in Neath changes, you are aiming for the B4434 towards Resolven). From Neath Railway Station, cross Windsor Road (one way system) onto Summerfield Place, the one way street between NatWest and Midland Bank.*
*At the T-junction **turn L** then at traffic lights **SA**. At second set of traffic lights **turn L**. At the small roundabout **bear R** onto the B4434 towards Resolven.*

2 *Go past the Post Office. Immediately after the cemetery on the right take the **next R** onto Fairyland Road 'Unsuitable for HGVs. Moss House'. This is a difficult turn on a left hand bend so it is preferable to go past the bend until you have a clear view of the traffic behind you before crossing the road.*

3 *Long steady climb. The views start opening up. Tarmac ends at power lines. Continue* **SA** *on the broad stone track (the left hand of the two tracks ahead) signposted 'Bridleway'. Enter forestry.*

4 *After 1 mile, at first X-roads of tracks* **turn L** *downhill then at fork* **bear R**. *(This fork is not marked on the map). Level section.*

5 *After 2 miles exit into clearing. At a X-roads of tracks follow the main track uphill to the right then take the first stone track* **sharply L** *across open grassland. Fine views to the left. Cross the open space. Go through metal bridlegate,* **bear L** *at fork signposted 'Dare Valley'. At the next fork* **bear L** *(in effect SA) 'Coed Morgannwg Way' (black footprint), 'Vale of Neath Walk' (blue arrow).*

6 *Lose height. After 3/4 miles* **turn R** *uphill on broad forest track. Climb, descend then climb again.* **Ignore** *two turns to the right (however the first of these right turns would drop you in Glyncorrwg to make this a circular ride via the Afan Valley and the B4287 back to Neath).*

7 *Climb steadily for 1 1/2 miles. Shortly after the brow of the hill and the start of the descent take the* **next L** *uphill. Follow the yellow bike waymarkings.* **Ignore** *a turning to the left. Climb to the summit of the ride, a X-roads of tracks by a red bike sign with a radio mast to the left. 1935 ft (590 mts).*

8 *At this point you have three options:*

a) retrace steps back to Neath.

b) **turn R** *downhill on the network of forestry roads to drop down into the Afan Valley near to Blaengwynfi. Follow the dismantled railway network southwest to Efail Fach then head northwest for 3 miles on the B4287 to return to Neath.*

c) **Main route** *continue on to Pontypridd. At the X-roads at the high point continue* **SA** *downhill. At T-junction by wooden signpost* **turn L** *'Red Bike Route' then at road (A4061 Treherbert to Hirwaun)* **turn L** *for 1/4 mile then* **1st R** *through green metal barrier into forestry.*

9 **Ignore** *turnings to right and left. Go past the Lluestwen Reservoir. The track turns to tarmac. Fast descent.* **Easily missed**, *shortly after the end of the stone wall and metal railings to the right leave the tarmac lane and* **turn L** *uphill onto track. First of two climbs on this second half of the ride.*

10 *At T-junction with road (A4233 Maerdy to Aberdare)* **turn sharp R** *for 1/4 mile then* **1st L**. *Second (and longer) of the two climbs on the second half of the ride.*

11 *Three miles after crossing the A4233, at major fork of tracks (GR 009978)* **bear R** *on the steeper of the two tracks.*

12 *After 2 miles, at T-junction with minor lane* **turn L** *then after 3/4 mile, on sharp left hand bend by the church in Llanwonno* **bear R** *on minor lane.*

13 *Follow this for 5 miles down into Pontypridd. At T-junction at the end of Rhondda Road* **turn L** *then* **R** *for Pontypridd railway station (Alternatively, follow the Taff Trail to Cardiff and catch a train to Neath).*

Pontypridd to Neath (east to west)

A *From the railway station in Pontypridd* **turn L** *and follow signs for the town centre. Immediately after passing a large church with a tall spire on the left* **turn L** *signposted 'Graigwen'. Climb steeply. At T-junction at the end of Graigwen Place* **turn R**. *Follow this road, climbing continuously between houses until reaching a cattle grid.*

B *Follow this lane for 4 1/2 miles.* **Ignore** *turnings to the right. At T-junction by the* *church and the Brynffynon pub in Llanwonno* **bear L** *to continue climbing. After 600 yards* **ignore** *first right turning into forestry (downhill track). Take the* **next R** *at X-roads of tracks to continue climbing to the first highpoint of the ride 1510 ft (460 mts).*

C *Descend gently over 2¹/₂ miles. Start climbing again. At T-junction with the road (A4233 Maerdy to Aberdare)* **turn R** *for ¹/₂ mile then* **sharply L** *through layby.*

D *Descend to the valley formed by Afon Rhondda Fach. At T-junction with tarmac lane* **turn R**. *At the dam by Lluestwen Reservoir* **bear R** *and climb steeply.*

E *After 2 miles, at T-junction with road (A4061 Treherbert to Hirwaun)* **turn L** *then take the* **1st track to the R** *by green metal barrier 'Rhondda Community Route'. Shortly, by large wooden signpost* **turn R** *'Red Bike Route'. Climb to the highpoint of the ride 1935 ft (590 mts) marked with a wooden signpost with both red and yellow bike signs. (There is a radio mast to the right).*

F **At this highpoint X-roads you have three options:**

1) retrace your steps back to Pontypridd.

2) **turn L downhill** *and use the network of forestry tracks to descend to the A4107 which you follow east as far as its junction with the A4061. Use forestry tracks to take you down into Tonypandy and the train (or road) back to Pontypridd.*

3) **Main route** *continuing on to Neath. Continue* **SA** *at the highpoint X-roads.* **Ignore** *the 1st right (opposite wooden signpost with yellow arrow). Follow the wide forest track around a sharp left hand then right hand bend, ignoring a left turn*

G *Fast descent.* **Ignore** *next left turn and* **shortly bear R** *uphill at fork. Climb then descend.*

H *At a T-junction by a low wooden post* **turn L** *gently uphill. Climb. Shortly after a wooden signpost marked with three blue*

arrows and a black footprint, as the main track swings left, **bear R** *(in effect SA) uphill.*

J *Exit woodland. Fast open descent with fantastic views. At T-junction with the edge of the forest ahead,* **turn R** *downhill and follow the main track round to the left to re-enter the forest.*

K *Long descent, great views. Short climb. At X-roads of tracks at the brow of this short climb* **turn R**.

L *Exit forest. Track turns to tarmac. Fast descent. At T-junction at the bottom of the hill at the end of Fairylands Road* **turn L** *downhill.*

M *At the roundabout* **bear L** *'Swansea/Abertawe' then* **1st R** *onto one way street passing the Cross Keys PH and aiming for the large church. At T-junction by the bus station* **turn L then 2nd R** *onto a road called Ropewalk.*
At X-roads by 'Give Way' sign **turn R** *onto the one way system to arrive at Neath railway station.*

▶ *Ride 1*

▶ *Ride 4*

▶ *Ride 4*

Ride 4 ◄

Ride 4 ◄

Ride 4 ◄

Ride 5 ►

Ride 5 ◀

Ride 6 ◀

Ride 6 ◀

THE ROUGH ROMAN ROAD OF SARN HELEN, ABOVE THE VALE OF NEATH

DISTANCE
12 miles (20 kms)

TIME
3 hours

GRADE
Moderate

TERRAIN
Wooded river valley, forestry and moorland. An old Roman Road

HILLS AND HIGHPOINTS
One major climb ▲ 1180 ft (360 mts) from the start to reaching Sarn Helen
Highest point ▲ 1245 ft (380 mts) at the junction with Sarn Helen
Total ascent ▲ 1400 ft (425 mts)

START
The National Trust car park by the Dulais Rock Inn in Aberdulais, northeast of Neath (GR 772994). Follow signs for Seven Sisters and Blaendulais from the A465 northeast of Neath

PARKING
The National Trust Car Park

NEAREST RAILWAY
Neath, 2 miles southwest of the start

REFRESHMENTS
Dulais Rock Inn, Aberdulais

Two rides in the book explore the old Roman road of Sarn Helen that used to run from Neath ('Nidum') to Brecon ('Cicucium').

Height is gained on either the quiet wooded lane leading north from Aberdulais (avoiding all but 1 mile of the busy A4109) or on good quality forestry tracks. After several wide sweeping bends the junction with the old Roman road is reached and soon the real fun begins as you drop over 1000 ft over the next 6 miles. The track undulates through forestry with occasional views down into the Vale of Neath. Once out of the woodland and after negotiating a couple of boggy sections views open up to both right and left, down into the Dulais valley as well as the Vale of Neath. The track steepens with the odd technical section before dropping though a mass of rhododendrons (beautiful in May/June) and popping out onto the road, out of the secret Roman kingdom and back into the present century.

WARNING! *The last section of the descent is very rough and may involve walking parts of it. For this reason it is also worth considering doing this ride in reverse (anti-clockwise) to leave you with a long descent on forestry then tarmac. See Ride 4 for anti-clockwise instructions for the start.*

1 *Exit the National Trust car park and* **turn L** *on the A4109. After 300 yards* **take the 2nd of two closely spaced left turns** *signposted 'Forest Hill leading to Cefn Yr Allt'. Climb steeply then leave the houses behind and follow delightful wooded lane on steady climb for 3 miles.*

2 *At T-junction with A4109* **turn L** *'Crynant' for 1 mile on this busy, unpleasant road. ¼ mile after passing the car park for Cefn Coed Colliery Museum take the* **next tarmac lane to the R** *'Crynant Forest'. Follow the track round to the right.*

3 *Long steady climb of 885 ft (270 mts) over 3 miles starting with a long sweeping left hand bend then passing through green metal barrier.* **Ignore** *turns to left and right, continue climbing steadily. At T-junction with the Roman Road of Sarn Helen* **turn R.** * *(The junction with Sarn Helen forms a 90 degree right angle and as such is unlike any of*

the other junctions you pass on the way up).

*** (For link to longer ride** *continuing northeast on Sarn Helen,* **turn L** *and follow Ride 4 Instruction 3 'Go past mast and quarry…').*

4 **Return to Aberdulais.** *Soon exit forestry with fine views into the Dulais valley and the Vale of Neath. Pass between drystone walls. At the ruin of a house* **bear L** *steeply downhill then shortly at X-roads with a broad stone track go* **SA** *through metal gate (red arrow).*

5 *Shortly* **fork L** *then at T-junction of tracks* **bear R** *on stony steep descent through rhododendrons. The bottom section is pretty rough and loose and you may prefer to walk. At T-junction with the B4242* **turn R** *then at T-junction with the A4109* **turn L** *to return to the start.*

SARN HELEN AND THE NEATH CANAL TO THE NORTHEAST OF NEATH

DISTANCE
Full route 20 miles (32 kms)
There-and-back route to highpoint
15 miles (24 kms)

TIME
Full route 4 hours
There-and-back route 3 hours

GRADE
Moderate

TERRAIN
Moorland, forestry, canal towpath,
old mining town (Dyffren Cellwen)

HILLS AND HIGHPOINTS
One main climb ▲ *1475 ft (450 mts)*
from the start to the highpoint, with one very
steep section at the start of the offroad section
Highest point ▲ *1580 ft (481 mts)*
Total ascent ▲ *1800 ft (550 mts)*

START
The National Trust Car Park by the
Dulais Rock Inn in Aberdulais, northeast of
Neath (GR 772994). Follow signs for Seven
Sisters and Blaendulais from the A465
northeast of Neath

PARKING
The National Trust Car Park

NEAREST RAILWAY
Neath, 3 miles from the start

REFRESHMENTS
Aberdulais, Dyffren Cellwen
and a Teashop on the canal towpath

**The old Roman road of
Sarn Helen, which used to run
from Neath ('Nidum' in Latin)
to Brecon is explored on two
rides in the book.
This one tackles the steep
stony climb head-on and having
reached the highpoint on the
plateau you are offered several
options which include returning
the way you came, dropping
down to the Neath Canal,
or taking a short cut down to
Cefn Coed Colliery Museum.**

The first part of the climb takes you across moorland between dry stone walls and sheep-grazed pastures with fine views alternating between the two valleys formed by the Dulais and Neath Rivers. Skylarks hover high up above the fern-covered hillsides and foxgloves lean out from the verges of the stone track as it climbs to almost 1600 ft. The descent towards the old mining village of Dyffren Cellwen is fast and furious and the section along the canal towpath is a gentle way to finish off the ride, although somewhat dominated by the noise from the A465. (There are hopes to restore the canal and its towpath along its entire length from Glyn Neath down to Briton Ferry).

1 *Exit the car park, **turn L** on the A4109 then after ½ mile **turn 1st R** on the B4242 'Resolven'. After further ½ mile and soon after passing beneath power lines at the end of a short dual carriageway section, keep an eye out for a rough stone track turning sharply back to the left by a 'No vehicles' signpost.*

2 *Much of the first 1¼ miles will be a push. Follow the main stone track steeply uphill, **forking L** after ¾ mile and continuing to gain height. At X-roads with a better track continue **SA** uphill (GR790007). Soon after the ruins of a stone house the gradient eases and is almost all rideable, crossing moorland.*

3 *Fine views down into the Vale of Neath and briefly into the Dulais valley. Enter the forestry. Go past mast and quarry. (**Short route.** 1½ miles after entering the forest take **1st major forest road L**. This is Ride 3 in reverse descending west to the A4109 south of Crynant).*
Main route.** Continue **SA** in the same direction. **Ignore** forestry roads to right and left. Climb to the second mast and then the second trig point. **At this point you have several choices:

a) make this a there-and-back ride and savour the descent on the Roman road.

b) extend the there-and-back route to Dyffryn Cellwen for refreshment in the unlikely looking pubs there.

c) follow the route described below with mixture of forestry tracks, canal towpath and road back to the start.

4 *   **Main route.** Continue **SA** from the trig point on a fast and stony descent to join a major forest road. **Ignore** the first left by green metal barrier with 'All Wards traffic' signpost. Follow the main forest road round to the left.*

5 *   **WARNING!** There are many more tracks on the ground than are marked on the map. You are aiming to descend to, then run parallel, with the power lines stretching off to the east. Go **SA** through two X-roads of forestry tracks as the main track swings round to the right and drops down to the power lines. The track turns to tarmac.*

6 *   Climb on tarmac, then once beyond the brow of the hill, the tarmac turns back to track. Superb fast descent. At the T-junction by a walled-in river **turn L** downhill.*

7 *   The track becomes tarmac. At the houses continue downhill, dog legging right then left at the end of Nant Hir. Go past chapel. At T-junction with the main road **turn R, then after 400 yards 1st R** 'B4242 Resolven'. After ½ mile take the **next road L** (no signpost) and after 150 yards keep an eye out for a **narrow path to the R** down to the canal 'Neath Canal Towpath'. Follow towpath for 3 miles.*

8 *   At the T-junction with the road, soon after the Ty Banc Cottage teashop **turn L**. At the roundabout with the A465 go **SA** then follow the B4434 for 3 miles through Resolven and Clyne.*

9 *   **Easily missed**, 1 mile after crossing a bridge over the railway and just after 'Oncoming buses' sign **turn R over narrow bridge, then L** alongside canal (GR798002). At a fork of tracks by a footbridge **bear L** alongside canal, then shortly take the stone bridge over the canal. Follow the track beneath railway bridge, **turn R** on the road by Railway Tavern then immediately after the traffic lights **turn R** following path beneath new dual carriageway back to the start.*

AFAN ARGOED AND THE PONTRHYDYFEN VIADUCTS

DISTANCE
12 miles (20 kms)

TIME
2½ hours

GRADE
Moderate

TERRAIN
Railway path, river valleys,
broadleaf woodland and forestry tracks

HILLS AND HIGHPOINTS
One major climb ▲ 920 ft (280mts)
from Efailfach to the highpoint in the forestry,
more than half on narrow tarmac lane
Highest point ▲ 1115 ft (340 mts)
Total ascent ▲ 990 ft (300 mts)

START
The Afan Argoed Countryside Centre, on the
A4107, 6 miles northeast of Port Talbot
(Jct 40 of the M4)

PARKING
The Afan Argoed Countryside Centre

NEAREST RAILWAY
Port Talbot, 5 miles southwest of the route
at Pontrhydyfen

REFRESHMENTS
Coffeee shop at the Visitor Centre
Colliers Arms, Efail Fach

Afon Argoed Countryside
Centre can be seen as the focal
point of mountain biking in the
southwest quarter of the
region covered by this guide.
Two rides start from the
Centre itself and there are a
further five rides within 6 miles.
This ride uses two magnificent
old stone viaducts in
Pontrhydyfen which cross the
Afon Afan.

Dismantled railways are used as far as Efailfach after which there is a steep climb on a dead-end tarmac lane with fine views opening up down into the valley. Just before the Mountain Centre the ride enters the forestry to continue climbing to a highpoint over 1100 ft. Just before the fast descent there are even better views up the valley. At the bottom of the hill you have the option of extending the ride to the east to take in more railway paths or of returning westwards to the delights of the Visitor Centre Coffee Shop.

1 From Afan Argoed Countryside Bike Hire Centre **turn L** onto tarmac path signposted 'Safety Notice–please push bike to cycle path' then shortly **fork R** onto paved path. Follow the path/track underneath the road bridge. At X-roads with railway path **turn L**.

2 At fork of tracks just after the Welsh Water brick building **bear R** downhill (the Forest Garden is to the right behind you). Cross bridge over river. **Bear L** through picnic site 'Pontrhydyfen 0.2 kms'.

3 At fork of tarmac lanes shortly after the picnic site **bear R** on the upper road (Pontrhydyfen is signposted to the left). **Turn L** over the viaduct 'Cyclists and pedestrians only'. At the T-junction at the end of the viaduct **bear R**. Go round sharp right hand bend.

4 Just after passing the church on the left and a school on the right, on a sharp left hand **bend bear R, then R again** onto tarmac path 'Efailfach 1.6 kms'. At T-junction at the end of the wall on the right, **turn L** downhill then shortly, at 3-way wooden bike signpost **turn R** to cross the last viaduct. At X-roads of tracks **SA** (GR 792943).

5 At T-junction with minor lane **turn R** then at T-junction with more major road (B4287) **turn R and shortly L** signposted 'Tonmawr'. After 1/2 mile, at the end of the houses **turn R** steeply uphill onto lane 'Unsuitable for HGVs'.

6 Steep climb on tarmac. Climb to the brow of the hill, start to descend towards the Mountain Centre then **turn R** just before buildings, taking the left hand of the two turns 'Llwybr Michaelston' and **bearing L** on the broad, steep track.

7 Keep climbing steadily, **bear R** at two forks (one minor, one major). At the third fork, shortly after the gradient eases (GR 826959) **bear R** again, this time downhill. Shortly follow the track downhill round a sharp right hand hairpin bend.

8 At T-junction at the bottom of the hill **turn R**.* After 2½ miles **take the first major track to the L**, turning sharply downhill by a 'Steep hill- cyclists dismount' signpost. Cross bridge over river, follow the track right then left, climb steeply, at X-roads of tracks go **SA** under bridge and follow back to the start.

** (**For extra loop**, taking in Cymer and optionally Glyncorrwg and Blaengwynfi, **turn L** here and join **Ride 6** at Instruction 4).*

AFAN ARGOED'S NETWORK OF EASY TRAILS

DISTANCE
Shortest ride 4 miles (6.5 kms)
Longest ride, 20 miles (32 kms)
with side trips, or much longer if you are
prepared to explore more of the forest

TIME
You should average at least 5-6mph on these
top quality tracks

GRADE
Easy!

TERRAIN
Valley railway path and
coniferous woodland

HILLS AND HIGHPOINTS
Gentle climb all the way up the valley
▲ 230 ft (70 mts)
climb from Visitor Centre to Cymer
▲ 490 ft (150 mts)
climb from Visitor Centre to Blaengwynfi

START
The Afan Argoed Countryside Centre, on the
A4107 6 miles northeast of Port Talbot
(Jct 40 of the M4)

PARKING
The Afan Argoed Countryside Centre

NEAREST RAILWAY
Port Talbot, 6 miles southwest of the
Visitor Centre

REFRESHMENTS
Coffee shop at Visitor Centre
Pubs in Glyncorrwg, Cymer and Blaengwynfi

*Afan Argoed will undoubtedly
become one of the real hubs
of recreational cycling in
South Wales. The whole area is
criss-crossed by railway paths
and forestry tracks.
One railway path leads to
the west over attractive stone
viaducts to Efail-fach and
Cwmafan and another leads to
the east towards Cymer,
Glyncorrwg and Blaengwynfi.*

From various points along the railway paths it is possible to link up with forestry tracks giving you access via offroad trails to places as far afield as the Neath Canal and the old Roman road of Sarn Helen in the Vale of Neath, Margam Forestry to the south and eastwards as far as Pontypridd (see Ride 2). For those seeking shorter, easier rides, Afan Argoed is perfect—there is a car park and a Visitor Centre with a coffee shop and plenty of waymarked trails starting right from the doorstep, with rides as short as 4 miles or as long as you want. As these closely follow the valley of the Afon Afan there are only gentle climbs on either side (with the one exception of the river crossing directly beneath the Visitor Centre). As a model of how old railways and mineral tramways could be turned into recreational assets it would be hard to improve on the example set here in the Afan valley.

1 From the Countryside Centre/Bike Hire Centre **turn L** onto tarmac path signposted 'Safety Notice—please push bike to cycle path' then shortly **fork R** onto paved path. Follow the path/track underneath the road bridge. At X-roads with railway path **turn L for Main route** (and the 4 mile loop to Cwm) or **SA** downhill for the 6 mile loop to Cymer.

6 mile loop to Cymer. Descend to cross river via bridge, follow the main track round to the left and climb steadily. At T-junction with broader track **turn sharp R** and rejoin the route at Instruction 4.

2 Main route and 4 mile loop. At fork of tracks just after the Welsh Water brick building **bear R** downhill (the Forest Garden is to the right behind you). Cross bridge over river. **Turn R through picnic site and R again** uphill passing through green metal gate waymarked with a yellow and green Forestry Commission bike sign to follow the parallel track back along the other side of the river.

3 After 1 mile at fork of blue and green routes stay on the main (lower) track. At the second waymarked fork by 'Steep hill-cyclists dismount' signpost **bear L**.*

* (4 mile loop back to the Countryside Centre. Bear R here, cross bridge over river, follow the track right then left, climb steeply, at X-roads of tracks go **SA** under bridge and follow back to the start).

4 Main route. The track climbs steadily and joins the road just after passing a blocked-up metal railway bridge to the right. Cross the valley via the next bridge (stone and concrete).
For an optional side trip to Glyncorrwg, just before crossing the river **turn L** and follow the broad track to the village at the top of the side valley. (It is also possible to go into the forestry via Glyncorrwg).

5 Main route. Cross the bridge over the river, follow the road to the left* then immediately **turn R** by the Fire Station towards the Refreshment Rooms PH.

* (Optional 5 mile extension on railway path to Blaengwynfi. Cross the bridge over the river, follow the road to the left then immediately **bear R** onto tarmac path just beyond Fire Station. Pass beneath bridge then take either track at the next fork—they both link after 3/4 mile. Go through gap in fence and continue on to Blaengwynfi, where you can once again access the vast tracts of forestry which extend miles to the north).

6 Return to start Gentle descent. After 3 miles and shortly after the caravan site and the stone barbecue shelter, go beneath bridge then take the **next L** beneath second bridge to return to the start.

MARGAM FOREST AND THE CWM DYFFRYN RAILWAY PATH

DISTANCE
15 miles (24 kms)

TIME
2 hours

GRADE
Moderate

TERRAIN
Broadleaf woodland, river valley, forestry

HILLS AND HIGHPOINTS
1st climb ▲ 850 ft (260 mts)
steady climb right from the start
2nd climb ▲ 195 ft (60 mts)
in the forestry, to the highpoint
Highest point ▲ 1115 ft (340 mts)
Total ascent ▲ 1310 ft (400 mts)

START
The far end of Wildbrook Road, Goytre
Port Talbot, ¾ mile east of M4 Jct 40
(GR 779897)

PARKING
From Junction 40 of the M4 take the A4107
east towards Cymer for a few hundred yards.
At the first mini-roundabout go straight
ahead (ie leave the A4107) then just before
the next T-junction turn L onto the housing
estate road called Wildbrook.
Park at the end of the estate.

NEAREST RAILWAY
Port Talbot, 1 mile from the start

REFRESHMENTS
Pub and stores in Bryn

*The starting point for this ride
is most unlikely–a neat housing
estate less than two miles from
the Port Talbot steel works.
However improbable it
may seem you will soon be
astonished at how quickly it is
all left behind as you climb
gently along the bed of an old
dismantled railway through
broadleaf woodland
alongside the picturesque
Ffrwd Wyllt river.*

Barely have you glimpsed civilisation again in the village of Bryn before you dive off into woodland once more, this time forestry plantation, as you climb on a series of sweeping bends up to a highpoint of over 1100 ft with magnificent views to the west towards Swansea. What goes up must come down and the descent is pretty much unbroken all the way back down to the start.

Time to move on–why not try the rides from Afan Argoed Countryside Centre, 6 miles northeast on the A4107?

1 *From the end of the housing estate road (Wildbrook) in Goytre, take the track that leads alongside the river, to the left of the garage. The track briefly joins a tarmac farm drive. Continue in same direction passing through gate to the right of farm buildings back on to gravel path.*
Follow for 3 miles as it climbs 330 ft (100 mts) through broadleaf woodland alongside the Ffrwd Wyllt river.

2 *At the end of the track with the housing estate in Bryn and a 'Cwm Farteg' signpost ahead **turn R** uphill towards the tarmac lane climbing between Station Terrace and Galltcwm Terrace. Follow the tarmac as it swings left through green metal barrier then sharply right.*

3 *Follow this main track as it climbs steadily on a series of broad sweeping bends with views opening up back down towards Bryn. Climb to the brow, descend briefly then continue climbing, with the track running parallel to the valley down to your right.*

4 *Reach a second summit and follow the main track downhill ignoring three turnings to the left then two closely spaced ones to the right. Start climbing again.*
***Ignore** one left turn. **Easy to miss**, at major fork of tracks (GR 828896) with the left hand track climbing more steeply and shortly forking again, **take the right hand track.** (If you want to make this into a longer ride you could add on an extra loop by taking the left hand fork and exploring the steep southern slopes of Margam Forestry).*

5 *Keep climbing to reach the highpoint of the ride with fantastic views behind and towards Swansea, passing between a line of redundant pylons along the firebreak running NW-SE. At the 1st X-roads after the start of the descent **turn R** gently uphill to recross the firebreak/line of pylons then shortly **turn L** downhill on the second of two closely spaced forestry roads.*
(This junction is by a triangle of grass with half a dozen trees in it; the main track swings round sharply to the right).

6 *At T-junction with stone quarry to the right **turn L**. (If you go up to the edge you will see a green lake down in the valley below). Fast descent. Follow the track around a right hand hairpin bend and along a line of beech trees. Descend to cross stream then **turn L** to continue downhill, (**or turn R** to visit the deep green lake/reservoir).*

7 *At X-roads with the minor lane go **SA** then immediately **turn L** onto the dismantled railway track for 2 miles back to the start.*

A MOORLAND AND FORESTRY CHALLENGE NORTH OF BLAENGARW

DISTANCE
13 miles (21 kms)

TIME
2¹/₂ hours

GRADE
Strenuous, particularly the first, rough push

TERRAIN
Moorland and forestry

HILLS AND HIGHPOINTS
*1st climb ▲ 1085 ft (330 mts)
from the start to the masts
at the head of the valley
2nd climb ▲ 1020 ft (310 mts)
from Croeserw to the highpoint in the forestry
Highest point ▲ 1805 ft (550 mts)
at the masts above Blaengarw
Total ascent 2460 ft (750 mts)*

START
*Beyond Blaengarw Hotel, at the end of the
Cwm Garw valley, A4064 north of Bridgend
(Jct 36 of the M4)*

PARKING
No specific car park

NEAREST RAILWAY
*Treorchy, 5 miles to the east of the route at
Instruction 4*

REFRESHMENTS
*Stores and pubs in Blaengarw, Blaengwynfi
and Croeserw*

*Blaengarw lies at the top of
the longest dead-end mining
valley in South Wales.
The ride starts where the road
ends and you are immediately
faced with one of the hardest
climbs (pushes) in the book to
the top of the steep moorland
slopes and the masts that
dominate the view from the
valley beneath.*

WARNING! The first section of this ride is a tough 25 minute push up a steep mountainside with little in the way of way-marking. It should only be undertaken by fit and experienced riders who know how to use a compass and should not be attempted in poor visibility, or in winter. You are aiming to join a good track just east of the radio masts on top of the hill.

This is by far the hardest section of the ride, all the rest of the route is on forestry tracks, dismantled railways or on road. Once into the network of forestry roads that lead off the A4107, almost any number of rides are possible–dozens of miles of tracks could take you west to Neath, east to Pontypridd or north to Glyn Neath and on to Sarn Helen, the old Roman road that continues as far as Brecon. The descent drops you down in the old mining village of Blaengwynfi and the dismantled railway path that runs down the valley of the Afon Afan almost to the M4 at Port Talbot. A second climb out of Croeserw sets you up for a fine forestry descent back to Blaengarw with some of the best views of the day.

1 From the top of Blaengarw, 200 yards after the last houses and just before the road crosses the main river which runs down the valley **bear R onto track towards bridlegate then immediately R** sharply back on yourself, away from the stony track, onto a grassy track alongside the fence.

2 Climb then contour. Just before a metal gate **turn L** sharply back on yourself to continue climbing up the hillside through several bridlegates. At the end of the well-made track aim for the bridlegate below the rocky outcrop.

3 The tough section begins! From this bridlegate continue **SA** uphill towards a ruined wall, **turn R** just before wall, go past an old gate post and continue in the same direction over a short boggy section. The track zig zags up the hillside. At best it is an obvious grassy track one metre wide. At worst there is nothing and you need to keep climbing in a northeast direction aiming just to the right of the radio masts.

4 Join a stone track close to the masts. This becomes a concrete track. At the road (A4107) **turn L** for 3/4 mile then on a sharp left-hand bend **turn R** through barrier onto forestry road 'Rhondda Community Route'.

5 At T-junction with a crescent-shaped clearing ahead **turn L then bear R** (GR 918964). **Easily missed**, on a fast descent, just before a wide sweeping left hand bend **take the 2nd of two closely spaced forest roads to the L**. Shortly, **bear L** at T-junction.

6 Fast descent. After 3 miles join tarmac at Gwynfi Street in Blaengwynfi. At T-junction with railings ahead **turn L** then at the next T-junction **turn R**. After 300 yards, just before left hand bend **bear R** onto tarmac path by metal railings/barrier.

7 After 1 1/2 miles, **exit via gap** in railings and join main road by row of low, terraced houses. **Turn R** on main road then after 300 yards take the **1st road to the L** turning sharply back on yourself.
At T-junction **turn R** then at Give Way (ie white lines across the road) go **SA**. After 300 yards **1st road L** by the telephone box.

8 Climb up through Croeserw. You are aiming for the corner of the forestry plantation. On a sharp right hand bend **turn L** onto Bryn Coed **then R** to enter the corner of the forestry. Go **SA** into forestry and shortly **fork L** (the right hand track leads to a farm).

9 Climb steadily. **Ignore** a left turn by a triangle of grass. Descend to cross stream. Start climbing and follow track round left hand hairpin bend. Keep climbing. At the next junction **bear L** to stay close to open field/moorland to the left.

10 At a fork of tracks after a long steady climb **bear L** alongside the field. Shortly after the start of the descent, **ignore** two closely spaced right turns (ie keep bearing left). Long descent down into Blaengarw.

OGMORE VALE, OGMORE FOREST AND MYNYDD WILLIAM MEYRICK

DISTANCE
14 miles (23 kms)

TIME
3 hours

GRADE
Strenuous

TERRAIN
Railway path, mountain pass, forestry, moorland

HILLS AND HIGHPOINTS
One long climb ▲ 1410 ft (430 mts) over 6 miles from the start to the highpoint on Mynydd William Meyrick (Instruction 6) Highest point ▲ 1700 feet (520 mts) on Mynydd William Meyrick (Instruction 6) Total ascent ▲ 1850 ft (565 mts)

START
The garage/Pub/Post Office and stores in Blackmill, at the junction of the A4093 and A4061, 4 miles north of M4 Jct 36

PARKING
Just beyond the Fox & Hounds PH and garage in Blackmill

NEAREST RAILWAY
Bridgend, 6 miles south of Blackmill

REFRESHMENTS
In Ogmore

This ride encapsulates much of the very best of mountain biking in the Welsh valleys. An old railway line serving the pit has been converted to recreational use and now runs for 7 miles from Nant-y-moel in the north down past Blackmill towards Bridgend in the south. The railway path is used at the start and end of the ride.

The middle section breaks into three parts: first the 600ft climb on one of the most spectacular roads in South Wales beneath the cliffs of Craig Ogwr; second the forest and moorland section climbing to a highpoint of 1700 ft then dropping to cross the headwaters of the Ogwr Fach before a fabulous forestry descent back to Ogmore. Along the way there are views down Ogmore Vale and the Vale of Glamorgan, and on a clear day, across the Bristol Channel to Exmoor. There are also fine views down into Rhondda, at one time the mightiest coal producing area in the world, and glimpses of the wind turbines set up on Mynydd Maendy, which may well represent a different future for power generation.

1 With back to the Fox & Hounds PH in Blackmill, **turn R** towards 'No through road' sign. Cross the river and **turn R** onto the railway path. Remember this point for your return route.

2 Follow the dismantled railway path for 5 miles, alongside the river, through broadleaf woodland then through Ogmore and up to Nant-y-Moel. The trail climbs gently and turns from tarmac to gravel.

3 At T-junction with the road at the very end of the trail in Nant-y-Moel, by a bridge over the stream with metal railings in a small green park (GR 934932) **turn R then 1st road L** sharply back on yourself just before the Nantymoel PH.

4 Climb steeply. At T-junction with the main road (A4061) **turn L** and follow this spectacular road for 2 miles. At the brow **turn R** uphill on broad forestry track by green metal barrier.

5 Climb steadily then gently. At the **1st junction bear R** (in effect SA). At the end of the stone track **turn L** through bridlegate to continue in the same direction on forestry track on the left hand side of the fence.

6 **Ignore** a left turn. Go past a large stone cairn near to the trig point and start descending. Stay on the main track as it swings around a sharp left hand then right hand bend. The stone base turns to black slag.

7 Easy to miss, keep eye out for forestry track to the R, soon after views of the valley of Tonypandy open up ahead. Follow this to its end and exit woodland. **Ignore** the track to the right which follows the woodland edge.

8 After 1/2 mile (GR 978917) **turn R** over the stile and walk your bike for 100 yards along the footpath to the grassy X-roads of tracks. **Turn R** on the grassy bridleway.

9 Descend to cross stream over smooth rock. Climb. The track becomes less distinct after the gate but as long as you maintain height and aim just to the left of the nearest clump of trees (heading roughly southwest) you will soon pick up a well-defined track.

10 At X-roads of tracks by the cattle grid **turn R** over the cattlegrid **then L** at the T-junction. On fast descent **bear L downhill at the 1st fork** (GR 957899).

11 Superb fast descent. At the next junction of tracks, cross the stream and follow the main track uphill to the left (ie **not** the minor track alongside the stream).

12 Climb steadily. A track joins from the right. **Ignore** turnings to the left (towards a farm) and to the right (into forestry). The track contours then descends.

13 Follow track down to the main road. **Turn R then 1st L** opposite the Fox & Hounds PH in Ogmore Vale. Shortly, at X-roads go **SA then 1st L** onto the railway path. Follow for 3 miles back to the start in Blackmill.

▶ *Ride 9*

▶ *Ride 10*

▶ *Ride 11*

▶ *Ride 11*

▶ *Ride 12*

▶ *Ride 13*

◀ *Ride 12*

▶ *Ride 13*

▶ *Ride 14*

▶ *Ride 14*

◀ *Ride 14*

Ride 15 ◄

Ride 15 ◄

Ride 15 ◄

10

A DOUBLE LOOP NORTH OF BRYNNA, BETWEEN THE RHONDDA AND OGMORE VALLEYS

DISTANCE
Two loops, of 8 miles (12 kms)
and 9 miles (14 kms) with a 1 mile linking
section, ie total of 19 miles (31 kms)

TIME
3¹/₂ hours

GRADE
Moderate

TERRAIN
Quiet lanes and farmland, wind turbines,
moorland, forestry

HILLS AND HIGHPOINTS
1st climb ▲ 740 ft (225 mts)
Brynna to Mynydd y Gaer (Instruction 3)
2nd climb ▲ 820 ft (250 mts)
from the crossing of the River Ogwr Fach
to the highpoint of the ride at the edge
of Ogmore Forest
3rd climb ▲ 460 ft (140 mts)
from recrossing River Ogwr Fach
to the wind turbines
Highest point ▲ 1280 ft (390 mts)
Total ascent ▲ 2625 ft (800 mts)

START
The Eagle Inn, High Street, Brynna
3 miles northeast of Jct 35 on the M4

PARKING
No specific car park–lots of space along
Brynna's main street

NEAREST RAILWAY
Porth, 6 miles from the route at
Instruction 4 (GR 975875)

REFRESHMENTS
Stores and pubs in Brynna
The New Inn, Glynogwr

*Lying just to the southwest
of Rhondda, one of the most
famous coal producing areas
the world has ever seen, this
ride perhaps shows a glimpse of
the future in the form of the
wind turbines producing
the energy that previously
needed to be dug out of
the ground.*

Wind turbines tend to divide people between those who see them as an ugly intrusion into beautiful upland areas and those who see them as a clean and green way of harnessing free power. Personally I can't see many nuclear accidents happening as a result of wind farms nor are many people likely to die of pneumoconiosis while maintaining the turbines. Explosions are unlikely and if we are talking of eyesores WHAT ABOUT PYLONS?! The southern loop is dominated by the wind turbines; the northern loop features farmland, an old mining community and some rough moorland tracks rising to over 1300 ft.

For shorter rides each loop could be taken individually or to lengthen the trip you could add extensions to the northern loop by linking with the tracks through Ogmore Forest in the west or the forestry holdings above Tonypandy to the north. Indeed, should you take the latter option and follow the forestry tracks northwest to the A4107 you will arrive, after a 2 mile stretch on road, at the start of an access road to the whole massive forestry block between the Vale of Neath and the valley of the upper Rhondda Fawr.

1 *With back to the Eagle Inn in the main street of Brynna* **turn R** *on to the road leading away from the High Street (Church Street). Descend then climb steadily, passing beneath power lines. At X-roads by Soar Chapel (your priority GR 972843) go* **SA**. *Descend then climb more steeply.*

2 *At X-roads with kennels/equestrian centre to the right (GR 946849) go* **SA** *to continue uphill. At the next farmhouse follow the road/track round to the right along the line of telegraph poles and shortly* **fork L** *onto narrower, rougher track 'Ridgeway Walk' (red arrow).*

3 *The broad stony track turns to grass. Keep climbing towards the wind turbines with fabulous views south over the Vale of Glamorgan and north towards Ogmore Forest. At the road* **turn L**.
(Short cut. *Cross road and continue towards*

the turbines, rejoin at Instruction 11 '…towards wind turbines.')

4 **Main route**. *Steep descent on tarmac. At T-junction with (busy) main road (A4093)* **turn R** *then after ¹/₂ mile, shortly after a large house with grey slate roof on the left take the* **next L** *on tarmac lane 'Bridleway.'*

5 *At fork by sign for Hendre Ifan Goch Farm* **bear L** *and climb.* **Easily missed**, *immediately before black metal gate and opposite wooden and corrugated iron barn to the left* **turn R** *downhill through overgrown section to cross bridge over stream.* **Bear R** *and climb. At T-junction with tarmac* **turn L** *through farm. Just before the last barn* **turn R** *uphill onto a broad gravel track.*

6 *Climb then descend. Immediately after double gates (field gate and bridlegate) adjacent to cattlegrid* **turn L** *uphill on broad stone track towards green metal barrier.*

7 *Follow the main track around sharp left hand then right hand hairpin bends, climbing steadily.*

8 **Easy to miss**, *soon after the brow of the hill, immediately before cattle grid and 30 yards before T-junction with wide forestry track,* **bear L** *alongside the fence and follow this round to the left, keeping the fence/wall to your right.*

9 *Follow the obvious track alongside wall. Pass through gate and follow the right hand field edge on less distinct grassy track. This soon becomes a walled, enclosed track.*

10 *Superb descent. Track turns to tarmac. Continue downhill. At T-junction with the main road (A4093)* **turn L** *for 1 mile. Shortly after crossing bridge over river take the* **1st road to the R** *through old railway bridge to rejoin outward route.* **Take care – this is a difficult right turn on a busy road.** *You are advised to continue past the turning until you have a clear view of the road behind you before crossing.*

11 *Climb for 1 mile. Just after the brow of the hill and a gravel parking area to the left* **turn L** *onto grassy track by three large*

boulders and a wooden signpost towards
wind turbines. Follow the 'Parish Road' signs
and blue arrows, passing the wind turbines,
also going through several gates.

12 The track deteriorates and will be
muddy in winter or after prolonged rain. At
X-roads of tracks by pylon **turn R** downhill.
At next X-roads of tracks **turn R then shortly
bear R** (in effect SA). The track improves on
the fast descent and turns to tarmac at the
farm.

13 At the T-junction at the start of
Brynna (GR 990834) **bear R** then at the
T-junction with the main road **turn R** again
to return to the start.

11

INTO THE FORESTRY ABOVE ABERDARE, BETWEEN THE CYNON AND TAFF VALLEYS

DISTANCE
15 miles (24 kms)

TIME
3 hours

GRADE
Moderate

TERRAIN
Forestry, moorland, sheep pasture, views of the industrial valleys

HILLS AND HIGHPOINTS
One major climb 1115 ft (340 mts) from Cwmbach to the upper slopes of Cefn Pennar
Highest point ▲ 1510 ft (460 mts) crossing Mynydd Merthyr
Total ascent ▲ 2115 ft (645 mts)

START
The railway station, Aberdare (M4 Jct 32–A470 towards Merthyr Tydfil, then A4059 towards Mountain Ash/Aberdare). Follow signs for Abernant and Cwmbach from the roundabout on the A4059 closest to Aberdare town centre

PARKING
Large car park near the Leisure Centre in Aberdare

NEAREST RAILWAY
Aberdare

REFRESHMENTS
Only in Aberdare

The Cynon valley is a 12 mile long urban ribbon from Abercynon to Hirwaun; the Taff valley is similar but stretches almost twice as far from Cardiff to Merthyr Tydfil. Meanwhile, up on the ridges, the forestry stands free of brick and mortar and you are more likely to see a sheep or a buzzard than a human being.

The ride heads southeast from Aberdare to Cwmbach before climbing steeply on the course of an old county road up to the mast. Tarmac is touched briefly close to the village of Cefnpennar before continuing the steep climb, across a stretch of moorland and into the forestry. Occasional views open out to the east down into the Taff Valley as the track continues northwards, dropping out of the forest then climbing once again to a second mast. This second highpoint sets you up for a descent of almost 1000 ft (305 mts) on a stony track then tarmac back to the start in Aberdare.

1 Follow signs for Abernant, Cwmbach and the General Hospital beneath the railway line to a small roundabout. **Turn R** here following signs for Cwmbach. **Easy to miss**, after $1^1/4$ miles, at the start of the houses in Cwmbach and opposite a petrol station **turn L** and follow this road as it swings right uphill.

2 Go past the Post Office, climb to the brow of the hill and take the **second of two closely-spaced left turns** onto Cefnpennar Road. **Ignore** several right turns. At a fork of tracks at the end of the tarmac, just past a house called Llettyshenkin, **bear L** on the steeper track and climb steeply through broadleaf woodland.

3 Follow the track past mast. Track turns back to tarmac. At the houses continue **SA** then shortly **fork R** onto the steeper and less-used of the two roads ahead. Follow the track past barn and through gate onto moorland. Cross the field/moorland climbing diagonally to the left. At the top of the climb as the track swings right and downhill **turn sharp L** to continue uphill, soon joining a more defined track.

4 Climb on this zig zag track past old steel cables embedded in the ground to enter forestry via gate onto narrow track and continue climbing. At top of a short steep push, at T-junction with major broad stone forestry road, **turn L,** then shortly at **fork of broad forestry tracks bear R** (this does not correspond with the map!) Follow this main, broad forestry track. **Ignore** turns to the left and right.

5 Go past a drystone wall on a sharp left hand bend. Views down to your right of the Taff Valley. The track undulates up and down over 4 miles. Exit forestry via a bridlegate next to green metal gate and **bear L** downhill.

6 The track turns to tarmac at the next gate. At X-roads at the end of Gernant Lane **turn L** uphill. (The Brecon Beacons loom on the horizon). Steep tarmac climb to the mast. Views of the Dare valley from the top. Fast stony then tarmac descent to return to the start.

12

CWM DARRAN COUNTRY PARK AND THE OLD MINING VILLAGE OF NEW TREDEGAR

DISTANCE
14 miles (22 kms)

TIME
2½ hours

GRADE
Moderate

TERRAIN
Country park, dismantled railway lines, old mining village of New Tredegar, moorland and forestry

HILLS AND HIGHPOINTS
One major climb ▲ 875 ft (267 mts) from the north end of Bargoed to the mast on top of the ridge
Highest point ▲ 1435 ft (437 mts) at the mast
Total ascent ▲ 1295 ft (395 mts)

START
Cwm Darran Country Park, northwest of Bargoed off the A469 between Caerphilly and Rhymney

PARKING
Cwm Darran Country Park

NEAREST RAILWAY
Bargoed or New Tredegar

REFRESHMENTS
Coffee shop at the Visitor Centre
Pubs in Bargoed and New Tredegar

Set between the valleys of the Rhymney and the Taff, Parc Cwm Darran perhaps shows a glimpse of the future. A well-equipped Visitor Centre with exhibitions and a good cafe is set in a landscaped area of lakes and newly planted broadleaf woodland. There are several short family bike trails including a dismantled railway converted to recreational use forming the start of this ride.

The railway path runs down the valley of the Nant Bargoed Rhymney as far as the northern tip of Bargoed before crossing the main Rhymney River and turning north along another dismantled railway through woodland. Before long you pass through the terraced houses of Brithdir and New Tredegar, so typical of the Welsh Valleys. Indeed, the steep climb up out of New Tredegar seems to encapsulate the Welsh Valleys in a nutshell: above you are the green slopes of the hillside, grazed by sheep and bounded by drystone walls. Below are the massed ranks of terraced houses clinging precariously to the slopes on the other side of the valley, representing a bygone age when the coal pits were in full operation and the majority of the houses would have had miners living in them. It is a mental task that occupied many hours of the time I spent researching the area to imagine what will become of these communities and villages in fifty or a hundred years. Back to the ride–the steep climb takes you up past a mast at over 1400 ft before droppng down through forestry back to the Visitor Centre.

1 From the Cwm Darran Visitor Centre **turn L** back up the hill towards the road for 50 yards then **1st L** through the overflow car park to join the cycle track. Follow this gently downhill for 2 miles. Cross the road in Deri by the Darran Hotel and continue **SA** for a further 1½ miles on the cycle track.

2 Continue in the same direction past the first houses in Bargoed. At T-junction with the High Street **turn sharply L** downhill. Cross the bridge over the river, start climbing steeply then **turn 1st L** onto Quarry Row. This becomes another dismantled railway path climbing gently towards New Tredegar.

3 At the end of the railway path (GR155017) at T-junction with lane **turn L** downhill to cross the river and pass beneath railway line. At 1st X-roads **SA** steeply uphill onto Herbert Street then shortly, at T-junction, **turn R** for 2miles.

4 At the X-roads by the Dynevor Arms **turn L**. At the top of the short climb,

ignore the first left on the A469 to Bargoed. **Shortly take the next lane to the L** (no sign), turning sharply back on yourself, by a tall stone wall. Climb steadily over 2 miles. Amazing contrast between the terraced houses of New Tredegar to the left and the green moorland to the right.

5 At T-junction at the top of the hill, shortly after a run-down farm on the left **turn R**. Continue **SA** in the same direction, as tarmac turns to track on left hand bend. Fine views. Go past isolated graveyard. The track turns back to tarmac and Rhymney looms ahead

6 Go past mast and a structure that looks like it has come out of a science fiction movie. **Easily missed**, after 2 miles as the descent steepens, with the terraced houses of Fochriw just ahead, on a sharp right hand bend **turn L** sharply back on yourself onto a broad stone track. Shortly **fork L** onto the upper, more defined track that climbs briefly before dropping to enter the forestry by a green metal barrier.

7 At X-roads with broad stone forestry track **turn sharp R downhill, then shortly 1st L**. At T-junction at the bottom of a fast downhill **turn R 'Ogilvie Lake' then L** over the wooden bridge to rejoin the cyclepath behind the stone-built toilet block. **Turn R** and follow the cyclepath back to the Visitor Centre.

13

THE CEFN MANMOEL RIDGE RIDE TO THE WEST OF EBBW VALE

DISTANCE
7.5 miles (12 kms) each way
15 mile (24 kms) round trip

TIME
2¹/₂ hours

GRADE
Moderate

TERRAIN
*Wooded tracks, quiet lanes, pasture
and fine views*

HILLS AND HIGHPOINTS
Two climbs on the outward leg
▲ *380 ft (115 mts)*
Two climbs on the return leg
▲ *200 ft (60 mts)*
Highest point ▲ *1535 ft (467 mts)*
Total ascent ▲ *1480 ft (450 mts)*

START
*Pen y Fan Pond Country Park, 3 miles
northeast of Blackwood, 3 miles southwest
of Abertillery*

PARKING
Pen y Fan Pond Country Park

NEAREST RAILWAY
*Bargoed, 5 miles southwest
of Pen y Fan Pond Country Park*

REFRESHMENTS
*Cafe at the Pen y Fan Country Park
Pub in the village of Manmoel*

*This is a fine linear
ride along the Cefn Manmoel
ridge that runs parallel with
Ebbw Vale in the east
and the Sirhowy Valley
in the west.*

Attempts to turn this into a circular offroad ride proved to be unproductive: the valleys either side of the ridge are heavily populated and carry busy roads. The next ridge along to the west is more appropriate, if you are happy to use a long stretch of tarmac, with a narrow lane running for 11 miles from Tredegar through Markham and Argoed back to the start. The ridge to the east of Ebbw Vale looks more promising from the map and indeed there are good tracks starting at the north end (near the golf course) and the south end (near Aberbeeg); however, the section in the middle is a 4 mile unrideable push over rough heather-clad moorland with no sign of the bridleway marked on the map. You have been warned! If you stick with the there-and-back option you will be rewarded with fine views in all directions, passing through a landscape seemingly untouched by the centuries of the iron and coal industry that have shaped the valleys below. Sheep graze pastures bounded by stone-walls and ancient hedgerows, there are fields of buttercups and stone-built farmhouses. The track is of fine quality along the ridge.

1 *Exit the Pen y Fan Country Park. At the road* **turn L,** *then after 300 yards, just after 30 mph signs* **1st L** *sharply back on yourself (to the left of Ty Dwr gate) onto stony track. Climb steeply.* **Ignore** *the track alongside the golf course. Shortly, take the next track to the right.*

2 *Climb over the brow of the hill with fine views ahead. At T-junction with road* **turn R** *'Manmoel'. Follow the next sign for Manmoel then by the triangle of grass* **bear R** *and follow this lane then track NNW for 6 miles, climbing to a highpoint just before the mast at 1535 ft (467 mts).*

3 *At the T-junction with the road between Tredegar and Ebbw Vale you have* **three choices**: *turn right to Ebbw Vale, turn left to Tredegar or return the way you came. This last option is by far the best as there are no good offroad options to form loops in either direction.*

Right to Ebbw Vale. *The bridleway on the ridge to the east of Ebbw Vale is non-existent for 4 miles south of Mynydd Carn-y-cefn. This section is a rough moorland crossing where you will have to push or carry your bike. The road alternative, the A4046 down the valley is very busy.*

Left to Tredegar. *Slightly better, although it is 11 miles on road. If you take the B4256 from Tredegar towards Rhymney then* **turn L** *on the lane at the top of the hill and* **turn L** *again after 3/4 mile you can follow lanes for 8 miles through Markham and Argoed to climb steeply back up to the Country Park.*

4 **Return route.** *Climb back past the mast to the highpoint. Descend, climb, contour, descend again. The track turns to tarmac. (You may wish to turn right into Manmoel for a drink at The Rhymney PH). Otherwise, continue past the turning to Manmoel, go round sharp right hand bend then after 1/2 mile* **turn L** *onto track signposted 'Mynydd Pen y Fan'.*

5 *Lovely row of beech trees. After 3/4 mile climbing, at fork of tracks* **bear R** *on the upper track. Climb to brow with wonderful views. Fine descent. At T-junction with road* **turn R,** *then after 300 yards R* **again** *into the Country Park to return to the start.*

14

COITY MOUNTAIN BETWEEN ABERSYCHAN AND ABERTILLERY

DISTANCE
20 miles (32 kms)

TIME
4 hours

GRADE
Strenuous

TERRAIN
Railway path, deciduous woodland, moorland, at times rough

HILLS AND HIGHPOINTS
1st climb ▲ 1200 ft (365 mts) over several miles from Abersychan to the highpoint of 1815 ft (553 mts) on the moorland above Abertillery
2nd climb ▲ 830 ft (250 mts) from the lake in Cwmtillery back to the highpoint
Total ascent ▲ 2460 ft (750 mts)

START
The free car park in the centre of Abersychan, 3 miles north of Pontypool on the A4043

PARKING
Free car park in the centre of Abersychan

NEAREST RAILWAY
Pontypool, 4 miles south of Abersychan

REFRESHMENTS
In Abersychan and Cwmtillery

There is quite a regular pattern to the landscape (and mountain biking options) in the old mining valleys of South Wales: the valleys tend to run north-south and are heavily populated; between them lie the unspoilt ridges where there are frequently good tracks.

On this ride, in the most easterly of the mining valleys of South Wales, access to the ridge is gained via a section of dismantled railway that will eventually be improved along its whole length from Blaenavon to Pontypool to link up with the canal towpath down to Newport forming part of the Sustrans National Cycle Network. Having risen above the valley the route continues climbing through broadleaf woodland and up to the moorland above Abertillery, reaching a highpoint of 1815 ft (553 mts). This is a 'roof of the world ride' over the moorland plateau, followed by a rough, unmarked descent down to Cwmtillery.

WARNING! *There is a short ($^3/4$ mile) rough descent across moorland to the north of Cwmtillery where there is no defined path. This is hard going but should present no real navigational problems as you are aiming to drop down into the valley where you will pick up a much better track. A compass is recommended. The ride should not be undertaken in poor visibility.*

Civilisation is only briefly touched before climbing back up to the moorland to repeat part of the outward route and finish with a fast descent back down to Abersychan.

1 From the car park in the centre of Abersychan, climb steeply on the B4246 (Union Street) signposted 'Tal y Waun, Garndiffaith'. Busy, unpleasant $^3/4$ mile climb. On sharp right hand bend with a railway arch ahead **turn L** sharply back on yourself onto The Promenade.

2 After 400 yards, on a sharp right hand bend **bear L** onto railway path. **Easily missed**, after 2 miles on the railway path **cross a stone bridge over stream**. Go under a round bridge then immediately after going beneath a square (newer) bridge **turn L through gate and L again** onto road that crosses the railway path.

3 At the top of a steep climb, opposite where a road joins from the left and just before a row of terraced houses **bear R** onto a track to the left of a wire fence. Wonderful broad, flat, stone-based track through beech trees.

4 At T-junction at the start of conifer plantation **turn L** uphill sharply back on yourself. At T-junction with road **turn R**. Follow this lane for $1^1/2$ miles. At T-junction with the mast ahead **turn R**.

5 After a further mile, on a sharp right hand bend soon after the end of the plantation on the right, take the **second of two closely-spaced tracks** (**not** the one to the ruined house) **to the L.** *

*** (For short cut**, missing out the Cwmtillery Loop. **Ignore the left turn** and continue along the road for 300 yards, **turn R** onto grassy track towards gate in wall then just before wall **turn L** onto grassy track alongside wall/fence. Rejoin at the last part of Instruction 11).*

6 **Main route**. The next section is repeated on the outward and return route. After 150 yards, at a X-roads of tracks by a small concrete water tank turn **sharp R** soon **forking L** to follow a grassy track parallel with the fence. The track becomes more defined.

7 At a fork of tracks with a forestry plantation just ahead and with the head of the valley to the left **bear R**. Stay on broad track, passing a 'Beware fissures' signpost. Descend to a X-roads with a better stone track near to small brick and concrete manhole (remember this spot as this is point to which you will return after completing the Cwmtillery Loop). At the X-roads go **SA** and follow this grassy track for 2 miles, descending then climbing to the highpoint at the head of the valley.

8 **Easily missed**, At the head of the valley, close to the top of the hill, just before the main track improves and becomes stone-based, **turn sharp L** onto faint grassy track.

WARNING! There is no real path for the next $^3/4$ mile on the descent down across the hillside into the valley below and the going is very rough and overgrown. Head due south *and ensure that you drop down into the Cwmtillery valley (**do not** stray west and drop down to Blaina). You are aiming to join a path alongside a wall in the flat valley bottom.*

9 *Follow the yellow arrows on an ever-improving path, maintaining height and joining a tarmac road. At T-junction at the bottom **turn L, then L again** to go past the bottom end of the lake. **Ignore** the left turn alongside the lake. Start climbing steeply, go round sharp right hand bend then take the **1st road L** sharply back on yourself alongside metal railings.*

10 *Climb steeply. After ³/4 mile, opposite a stone and corrugated iron barn **turn R** onto steep broad stony track, just after the side valley on the right. **Easily missed**, at the brow of the hill with faint grassy tracks to the right and left **turn R** to rejoin the outward route. Shortly, at fork **bear R**.*

11 *Climb then descend. Go past forestry to the right. At the next fork **bear R** parallel with the fence. At a littered X-roads of tracks near to a concrete water tank **turn L** towards the road. At the road **do not** take the obvious track opposite. **Turn L** on the road for 300 yards then **turn R** onto grassy track towards gate in wall. **Do not** go through gate but **turn L** alongside the fence / wall.*

12 *The grassy track contours, briefly climbs then becomes a fast descent. At X-roads with first wide gravel track go **SA**. Shortly, at X-roads with second gravel track **turn L**, then at gate **turn R** downhill. At T-junction with Pentwyn Post Office ahead **turn L**.*

13 *At T-junction with B4246 at the end of The Promenade **turn R** sharply back on yourself to return to the start in Abersychan.*

15

THE TAFF TRAIL BETWEEN CARDIFF AND MERTHYR TYDFIL

DISTANCE
*30 miles (48 kms)
from Cardiff to Merthyr Tydfil
60 miles (96 kms) round trip*

TIME
4 hours one way

GRADE
Easy

TERRAIN
*Riverside path, woodland,
fringe of industrialised valley*

HILLS AND HIGHPOINTS
*The ride climbs steadily from Cardiff (at sea
level) to Merthyr Tydfil ▲ 655 ft (200 mts)
The most notable climb apart from this gentle
uphill gradient is the very steep push either
side of Castell Coch*

START
*Railway Station, Cardiff
Music and Drama School North Road, Cardiff
Rhydycar Leisure Centre, Merthyr Tydfil
Railway Station, Merthyr Tydfil*

PARKING
*Railway Station, Cardiff
Music and Drama School North Road, Cardiff
Rhydycar Leisure Centre, Merthyr Tydfil
Railway Station, Merthyr Tydfil*

NEAREST RAILWAY
*Cardiff, Merthyr Tydfil and railway stations
all along the route*

REFRESHMENTS
All along the route

**Opened in 1995 and
running from Cardiff through
Merthyr Tydfil to Brecon, the
55 mile Taff Trail now forms
part of the Sustrans National
Cycle Network which continues
beyond Brecon right the
way across Wales and
up to Anglesey.
This 30 mile section offers a
magnificent exit from the
very heart of Cardiff and links
together some fine offroad
trails alongside the River Taff.**

With stretches of dismantled railways running high above the busy industrial valley below the ride shows the contrasting faces of South Wales: the densely populated valleys below and the generally unspoilt ridges and hills which lie above them. Should you continue north to Brecon, the industrial aspect is left behind and you enter a landscape shaped by reservoirs, forestry and sheep farming. The route is in general signposted to a very high standard, either as the Taff Trail or as Sustrans National Cycle Network Route Number 8. However, as a belt and braces approach, the route is also described below in both directions from the railway stations at either end. The best option would be to catch a train from Cardiff to Merthyr Tydfil which lies at 200 mts (660ft) above sea level and follow gravity back downhill to Cardiff.
The most scenic section lies between Cardiff and Castell Coch and the 6 miles north of the castle (Instructions 1-7).

1 *Exit Cardiff Railway Station* and* **turn L**. *At the traffic lights by the Empire Pool* **turn L** *then immediately after crossing the bridge over the river* **turn R** *(use the pelican crossing) and follow the pavement northwards alongside the river.*
During the course of the ride you will be following one of two sorts of sign: 'Taff Trail' or the white, blue and red logo indicating Sustrans 'National Cycle Network 8'.

** (**Alternative start from near Cardiff Castle**. From the College of Music and Drama on North Road (just north of Cardiff Castle on the A470 towards Merthyr Tydfil) follow signs for the Taff Trail, parallel to and to the east of North Road. You will soon find yourself alongside the River Taff. At a fork of tracks after 3/4 mile, pass to the left of a black and white timbered lodge house and follow the riverside path. Rejoin at Instruction 3).*

2 *At a round stone pillar and Taff Trail sign* **turn L away from the river, then shortly R** *along a wide tarmac avenue. Exit parkland via ornate gates and* **turn R** *along the pavement to cross the bridge over*

the river. At the end of the bridge **turn R down steps, then sharply L** *to follow the riverside track.*

3 *Go past a weir and alongside playing fields,* **bear R** *away from the river at the Taff Trail signs then briefly use the shared pavement alongside the road.*
After 3/4 mile, as the road starts climbing on a right hand bend, immediately after an old metal and wooden water pump, **turn L** *onto tarmac track between newly-built houses to return to the track alongside the river.*

4 *Briefly use a minor road, continuing in the same direction alongside the river. At a T-junction of tracks by a pylon* **turn L** *and pass beneath the M4.*
Join a minor lane and follow this beneath a second viaduct (the A470). At the T-junction at the end of Iron Bridge Road in Tongwynlais **turn L** *then after 400 yards* **turn R** *by the Lewis Arms PH onto Mill Road.*

5 *Follow for 3/4 mile then* **turn L** *at the sign for Castell Coch. Steep climb on tarmac. Opposite the castle itself* **turn R** *onto track signposted 'Taff Trail' that soon becomes very steep and will involve a push. At T-junction at the top* **turn L** *to continue climbing gently before a fast descent through woodland.*

6 *Join the track of an old railway. Fine hill views ahead. At the end of the level track, briefly join a downhill tarmac track that becomes a lane. Shortly,* **bear L** *onto another railway track. At fork after 1/2 mile by bridge over track* **bear L** *uphill.*

7 *The tarmac track climbs to cross the A468 dual carriageway via a pelican crossing.* **Go L then R** *onto Heol Y Gors and shortly take the* **2nd of two closely spaced roads to the R**, *following 'Taff Trail/Pontypridd' signs to rejoin a railway path through a woodland setting.* **(For a short route**, *avoiding an unpleasant section on the A4054, follow the railway path as far as the next road (kids' playground ahead, pylon to the left) then turn around and return to your starting point).*

8 **Continuation northwards**. *Cross road and pass through a run-down housing estate.*

Go past a cemetery (on your right). Join a tarmac lane, **turn L**, then at the T-junction with the main road (A4054) **turn R**.

9 After 1½ miles climbing gently on this busy road **turn L** signposted 'Trallwng'. Pass beneath the bridge then shortly, on sharp left hand bend **turn R**. At the end of the terraced houses bear left downhill and follow track through fields and near to the river. Cross a new wooden bridge bridge over a side stream. At T-junction with broad track with tall wire fence ahead **turn R** then follow it round to the left as it turns to tarmac, passes through the industrial estate and crosses the A470 via a bridge. At T-junction with the A4054 **turn L**.

10 At the traffic lights after 1½ miles **turn L** 'Abercynon B4275' then shortly, at second set of traffic lights **turn R**. On a sharp left-hand bend shortly after the Navigation Inn **turn R** 'Single track road. Tramroadside'.

11 Pass beneath two large road bridges. The lane turns to a narrow track. Cross the river (the track turns back to tarmac). Pass between terraced houses and go **SA** at X-roads. Tarmac becomes track once again. Lovely woodland section. At T-junction with road at the end of the track **turn L**. Cross small bridge, pass beneath A470 on stepped subway then **turn sharply R** at the top and follow lane parallel with main road for 1½ miles.

12 Pass back through subway. **Easily missed**, on the descent shortly after the end of the wooden fence on the left **turn sharply L**. Follow this obvious track/tarmac path/lane for 5 miles to the Rhydycar Leisure Centre on the outskirts of Merthyr Tydfil.

The Taff Trail through Merthyr Tydfil is at present fairly unpleasant, although improvements are scheduled. For Merthyr Tydfil railway station leave the Taff Trail by Rhydycar Leisure Centre, cross the bridge over the river then go **SA** at the first roundabout then left at the second roundabout.

The Taff Trail North to South. (Merthyr Tydfil Railway Station to Cardiff Railway Station).

A Exit Merthyr Tydfil railway station, **turn R**. At the roundabout **turn R** downhill then at the next (major) roundabout go **SA** 'Rhydycar Leisure Centre'. Cross the bridge,

turn L down steps and **bear L** to join the Taff Trail, to the left of the red-brick building 'No Unauthorised Vehicles'.

B Follow obvious track/tarmac path/lane for 5 miles in the same direction, passing through Upper Abercanaid, Abercanaid and Aberfan. At T-junction at the end of the track, with metal railings ahead **turn sharply R** uphill to pass beneath viaduct

C **Easy to miss**, after 1½ miles, shortly after a metal barrier by a house on the left **turn sharply L** downhill at a junction of tracks/roads near to a pylon (GR 079975). Stepped subway beneath the A470. Cross the stream, start climbing steeply then take the **1st track to the R** through a gate. Lovely woodland section.

D Track turns to tarmac. At X-roads with lane go **SA**. The track narrows and descends to cross bridge over river. It soon widens again, turns to tarmac and passes beneath two huge road bridges.

E At T-junction with busier road **bear L** past the Navigation Inn. At the first traffic lights **turn L** then shortly, at the next traffic lights **turn R** on the A4054 towards 'Cilfynydd'. Gently downhill for 1½ miles. Pass beneath two closely-spaced power lines then take the **next road R** 'Albion Industrial Estate'. Follow the road through the industrial estate and round to the right. Shortly after tarmac turns to track **turn L** onto a narrow path 'Taff Trail'.

F Pass alongside the river. Cross a new wooden bridge. The track turns to tarmac, climbs and passes along a residential road. At the T-junction at the end **turn L** beneath viaduct. At T-junction with A4054 **turn R** 'Glyntaff'. After 1½ miles take the **1st major road L** signposted 'Glyntaff Crematorium'. Shortly after the start of the cemetery on the left **turn R** onto narrow path 'Taff Trail.'

G Go past housing estate. At X-roads with road immediately after kids playground go **SA** onto railway path. At the end of the track follow signs to cross the busy A468 via the pelican crossing.

H Descend then continue in same direction as the railway path joins a tarmac lane, climbs and rejoins another railway path. At the barrier at the end of the railway path climb steeply through woodland. Shortly after the brow of the hill and the start of a gentle downhill **turn sharply R** for a steep descent to Castell Coch. At T-junction with the castle ahead **turn L**.

J At the T-junction with minor lane at the bottom of the castle drive **turn R** downhill. At the T-junction at the end of Mill Lane near to the Lewis Arms PH **turn L** then after 400 yards **turn R** onto Iron Bridge Road. Follow the road beneath the viaduct as it swings right.

K At the end of the tarmac **bear L** onto a riverside path. Pass beneath the M4 then shortly **turn R** immediately before a pylon, signposted 'Taff Trail'. Lovely wooded river stretch. The Trail briefly uses a minor lane, continuing in the same direction, before rejoining the riverside path.

L Follow Taff Trail signs as the route swings left away from the river (by a barrier/white line) passing between newly-built houses to join a shared-use pavement near to the old Melingriffith Water Pump. After ¾ mile **turn R** to re-enter parkland on a track running past football and rugby pitches and rejoin riverside path.

M **Easy to miss**, You need to cross the river via a wide, stone-built road bridge with round, ornate balustrade supports. **Pass beneath this bridge then turn sharp R* to get up onto the bridge.** Cross the river and take the **1st road to the L** a no through road signposted 'Taff Trail'. After ¾ mile on this wide tarmac avenue **turn L** onto a track alongside a stone wall. Rejoin the riverside path.

* (The route along the left hand side of the river leads to Cardiff University and Castle).

N Cross the busy Cowbridge Road via a pelican crossing. At the next main road (also with a pelican crossing) **turn L** and get into the right hand lane to return to Cardiff railway station.

▶ *Ride 16*

▶ *Ride 16*

▶ *Ride 17*

Ride 17 ◀

Ride 18 ◀

Ride 19 ◀

Ride 17 ▶

Ride 21 ◀

Ride 20 ◀

Ride 20 ◀

16

INTO THE HILLS EAST OF CASTELL COCH

DISTANCE
15 miles (24 kms)

TIME
3 hours

GRADE
Moderate

TERRAIN
Woodland, broadleaf and coniferous, farmland

HILLS AND HIGHPOINTS
1st (steep) climb ▲ 230 ft (70 mts)
up from Castell Coch
2nd (steady) climb ▲ 560 ft (170 mts)
from Machen to the highpoint
on the Ridgeway
Total ascent ▲ 1690 ft (515 mts)
Highest point ▲ 820 feet (250 mts)

START
Castell Coch car park, near Tongwynlais,
north of Cardiff. (GR 131825)
Follow signs from Jct 32 of the M4

PARKING
Castell Coch car park

NEAREST RAILWAY
Caerphilly or several of the urban stations
in north Cardiff

REFRESHMENTS
Rudry Village Inn, west end of Rudry
Maen Llwyd Inn, east end of Rudry

*The woodland between
the M4 and Caerphilly is criss-
crossed by bridleways and
contains the best concentration
of quality mountain biking
tracks close to Cardiff.
An added bonus is that the
ride can easily be accessed by
following the excellent Taff Trail
from the very heart of Cardiff
as far as Castell Coch then
diving off into the woods
to join up with the route
described below.*

For somewhere so close to a major city, this ride has a very secluded, rural feel to it with a wide variety of broadleaf trees notably beech, hazel, hawthorn and ash. Sheep graze the pastures and but for the very occasional traffic noise rumbling up from the M4 and the view down towards Caerphilly from the ridge one could be forgiven for believing that the ride was set in a much more remote part of Wales.

1 *From the Castell Coch car park follow Taff Trail signs opposite the castle onto a track that climbs very steeply through woodland. At the junction at the top of the climb, leave the Taff Trail and continue* **SA**.

2 *After 1½ miles, at T-junction with road* **turn L** *uphill, then at the next T-junction* **turn sharp R**. **Ignore** *left turn into quarry. After 600 yards, immediately after a white cottage to the left,* **turn L** *by a triangle of grass and wooden bridleway signpost onto broad stone track.*

3 *Climb and descend through broadleaf woodland. Go past ruins and continue* **SA** *through left hand of two gates onto rougher track. Soon,* **at fork take the lower right hand track**. *Cross stream, go through gate and across golf course, passing to the right of the golf course buildings.*

4 *At T-junction with main road (A469)* **turn L then R** *through gate to pass to the left of the farm. Follow in the same direction on good track (with one muddy section). At T-junction of tracks* **turn L** *uphill onto narrow stony track following the blue arrows (remember this point for the return trip).*

5 *Shortly, at the fork of tracks by field gate and bridlegate the outward and return routes split.* **Bear L** *downhill on fast gravel descent.* **Easily missed**, *immediately after the start of the concrete track on the climb* **bear L** *onto track (blue arrow).*

6 *Go through clearing with fine views of Caerphilly and its castle to the left. At a fork of tracks with a stone barn in a clearing to the left* **bear R** *on the upper track. At a five-way junction of tracks continue* **SA**.

At T-junction with a small lane **turn L**.*

* (First short cut, turn R here, climb steeply. Immediately after farm on left **turn R** *through bridlegate adjacent to field gate. Rejoin route at second part of Instruction 13, 'At T-junction by a wooden post...').*

7 *At T-junction with a broader lane by triangle of grass* **turn L then R** *onto a track marked by a wooden bridleway sign.* **Fork R** *by the picnic tables onto the track along the right hand slope of the hillside ahead. Climb then descend.* **Do not** *go through the gate ahead but follow the bridle-way round to the left alongside fence / line of trees then round to the right, crossing one boggy area.*

8 *At T-junction with lane* **bear L**. *At X-roads with Pentwyngwyn Road* **turn R**. *After ¾ mile* **turn L*** *on the road by Rudry Primary School, signposted 'Machen 2½'.*

* (Second short cut, go **SA** *here then after ½ mile at T-junction with the main road go* **SA** *onto the upper forestry track opposite and rejoin route at Instruction 12, 'After 100 yds* **bear R** *on the upper gravel track...').*

9 **Main route**.
Ignore *a forestry track to the right, shortly,* **bear R** *at fork of lanes. Climb then descend.* **Easily missed**, *200 yds after a house called 'Cats Haven' to the left,* **on a sharp left hand bend bear R** *onto track then after the gate* **bear L**, *following the fence. Where the fence turns sharp left with a wide field ahead* **bear R** *aiming for a point between the masts and the quarry on the horizon towards an indented 'corner' formed by the woodland.*

10 *Cross the stile (it is a bridleway, honest!). Keep bearing left on improving track. At T-junction with gravel track soon after a house on the left* **turn R**. *At T-junction with tarmac* **turn R** *then after 200 yards* **turn R** *again onto a track towards a metal gate and bridlegate.*

11 *Follow this well-made track on long, steady climb then long undulating section.* **Ignore** *turnings to right and left. At the road by the 'Llwyn Hir' Forestry Commission sign* **turn R**.

12 *Shortly after the Maen Llwyd Inn, and opposite the second of two closely spaced lanes to the right,* **turn L** *sharply back on yourself onto the upper forestry track. After 100 yards* **bear R** *on the upper gravel track then shortly* **fork R** *again.*

13 *Lovely woodland section with one steep push. Even better views particularly down towards Caerphilly. At the road by the farm go* **SA**. *At T-junction by a wooden post* **turn R downhill, then shortly L**.

14 *Rejoin the outward route by a field gate/bridlegate.* **Easily missed. After 100 yards of descent turn R.** *Follow the track above the farm to the main road (A469).* **Turn L then R** *onto track. Cross golf course,* **bear R** *at the fork at the end of the course onto a narrow grass track ('Private path to the left). Through gate. Cross stream.*

15 *The track improves. At T-junction with road by a triangle of grass* **turn R, then take the 1st road L**. *Shortly, take the forestry track to the right and follow for 1¹/₂ miles. As the track swings right by a Taff Trail sign* **bear L** *steeply downhill to Castell Coch.*

17

SIRHOWY VALLEY COUNTRY PARK AND THE RHYMNEY VALLEY RIDGEWAY

DISTANCE
12 miles (20 kms)

TIME
2¹/₂ hours

GRADE
Moderate

TERRAIN
Woodland, moorland, railway path

HILLS AND HIGHPOINTS
One climb ▲ 935 ft (285 mts)
mostly on tarmac, at times very steep
up from Crosskeys
Highest point ▲ 1130ft (345 mts)
Total ascent ▲ 1295 ft (395 mts)

START
The Full Moon Visitor Centre in
the Sirhowy Valley Counrty Park, just off the
roundabout west of Risca at the junction of
the A467 and the A4048
OS Landranger 171 (GR 215914)

PARKING
The Full Moon Visitor Centre

NEAREST RAILWAY
Ystrad Mynach

REFRESHMENTS
Islwyn Inn, Halfway House PH, Wyllie
Ynys Hywel Coffee Shop on the railway path
Open weekends 1200-1700 hrs
(April to September)

The Sirhowy Valley Country Park has waymarked mountain bike trails in addition to the ride described below. There are signboards at the entrance to the park indicating where these are to be found.

The ride starts by getting the least attractive section out of the way: 1¹/2 miles through Crosskeys to the start of Black Vein Road. This steep tarmac climb leads onto the road / track used by the Rhymney Valley Ridgeway Walk, a long, circular walk that links the ridges between the industrialised valleys in the heart of the mining area. The views from the top are panoramic although occasional spoil heaps to the west and traffic noise coming up from the valleys remind you that you are still in the heart of a highly populated area. A fast road descent takes you back down to the railway path that leads alongside the river back down to the start.

WARNING! The railway path is popular with walkers. Please show consideration when passing. Make a noise to let walkers know you are coming–try a 'Good morning' or 'Good afternoon', whistle, sing, cough, 'clack' your brakes, 'ping' your brake cable against the frame. Thank people who step aside for you and remember what it is like when a car shows you courtesy when you are on your bike.

1 *From the Sirhowy Valley Country Park Full Moon Visitor Centre at GR 215914 return to the A4048 / A467 roundabout.* **Take the 1st exit (A4048) then 1st R** *'Newtown Industrial Estate'. Cross the river then take the* **1st R** *onto Cobden Street.*

2 *After ³/4 mile take the* **1st road R** *(Black Vein Road). Cross the river, pass beneath major road bridge and then* **fork R** *to start the big climb.*

3 *Follow the road steeply to the top. Descend then climb twice along the ridge section. Cross a cattle grid then leave the tarmac lane,* **bearing L** *uphill on broad stone track towards a second cattlegrid.*

4 *Follow the track for 4 miles, leaving the forestry to your right then aiming for the white-topped mast. At a three way split of tracks just before the mast* **bear R.** *Fast tarmac descent.*

5 **Easily missed,** *1¹/4 miles after the mast and just before the Brynmeadows Golf Club*

take the second lane to the R *'Wyllie 1'.* **Second easily missed turn,** *on fast downhill take the* **1st road to the R** *by 'Islwyn Inn' sign.*

6 *Go through Wyllie. At the end of the houses* **bear L** *onto the broad railway path and follow this for 5 miles back to the start.*

18

EASY RIDING ON THE TWO CANALS NORTH OF NEWPORT

DISTANCE
Newport to Crosskeys 7 miles (11 kms)
one way / 14 miles (22 kms) round trip
Newport to Pontypool 9 miles (14 kms)
one way / 18 miles (29 kms) round trip

TIME
Newport to Crosskeys 1 1/2 hours one way
Newport to Pontypool 2 hours one way

GRADE
Easy!

TERRAIN
Canal towpath through woodland
and built-up areas

HILLS AND HIGHPOINTS
Surprisingly, there are short, steep hills on
both canals! There is a 260 ft (80 mts)
climb from Newport to Crosskeys and a
295 ft (90 mts) climb to Pontypool

START
Malpas Road (A4042), Newport
(GR 308892). From M4 Jct 26 take the
A4042 south towards Newport then park in
one of the side streets to the right (Goodrich
Crescent, Ross Lane, Walford Street)

ALTERNATIVE START
The free car park in the centre of Crosskeys
(GR 221918), 6 miles west of Newport near
the junction of the A467 and the A4048

PARKING
Goodrich Crescent, Ross Lane, Walford Street
The free car park in the centre of Crosskeys

NEAREST RAILWAY
Newport, Cwmbran, Pontypool

REFRESHMENTS
Pubs and stores just off the route

*These two canals both
form part of Sustrans Grand
Strategy for South Wales.
The Newport to Crosskeys
route will continue westwards
along the Sirhowy Valley and
through Pontllanfraith to join
the Taff Trail in Pontypridd.
The Newport to Pontypool
route will be extended to
Abersychan, Blaenavon and
eventually swing east towards
Abergavenny.*

Unfortunately the eastern branch can only be ridden as far as the north end of Pontypool. Beyond this, the towpath through to Brecon is not open to cyclists although this is a situation which may change in the future. There is a section through Cwmbran where the canal has disappeared – follow instructions carefully. The western branch to Crosskeys is the more scenic of the two canals, with picturesque hump-backed bridges, fine woodland stretches and good views of hills rising to over 1000 ft on either side. This, in spite of the somewhat unlikely start from Newport when the canal runs alongside the M4 for almost 2 miles. After this the canal rises steeply up a series of locks (now disused) and runs along a remarkably green corridor through Risca to Crosskeys. In Crosskeys you can either return directly or explore the block of forestry lying to the north (Cwmcarn) or Sirhowy Valley Country Park to the west.

1 *Starting from Newport.*
Follow Malpas Road for 200 yards south as far as the pedestrian bridge over the road. At this point **turn R and keep bearing R** to join the start of the canal towpath. Pass beneath a bridge then shortly you have a choice. At the next new stone bridge **turn R** beneath the M4 for **Pontypool** or continue **SA** for **Crosskeys**.

2 *Towards Crosskeys.*
Noisy section alongside the M4. Pass beneath the motorway and climb steeply past the fourteen locks. Fine views towards the hills. The canal occasionally stops– continue in the same direction and you will rejoin it shortly. At X-roads with more major road go **SA** onto Darren Road and follow it round to the left to rejoin canal.

3 *The canal ends at GR 219931.* **At this point you have several choices:**

a) retrace your steps back to Newport

b) head east to explore the forestry tracks to the east of Cwmcarn

c) join up with the railway path through

the Sirhowy Valley. This is described below in Instruction 4

d) link with **Ride 17*** which climbs up to the Ridgeway Path before descending to Wylllie and back along the railway path.

4 *From the end of the canal path retrace your steps for $1/2$ mile then leave the towpath at the first bridge (GR 220925) and **turn R** (ie south) downhill towards Crosskeys. At the traffic lights go **SA** through Crosskeys town centre.* At the T-junction with the main road (A4048) **turn L** towards roundabout then **take the 3rd exit** signposted 'Sirhowy Country Park'. Follow this road/railway path for 4 miles as far as Wyllie.*

** (To link with Ride 17 go SA at the traffic lights then **take the second L** onto Cobden Street and join the other ride at Instruction 2).*

5 *Starting from Crosskeys.*
Leave the car park (GR 221918) **turn L** then at the traffic lights go **SA** beneath the railway bridge onto the B4591 signposted 'Pontywaun $1/2$'. Go past the Crosskeys Hotel, cross the railway bridge then **turn R** immediately to join the canal towpath. Follow for 7 miles into Newport.

6 *Newport to Pontypool*
(From the junction of the two canals near Newport at GR 303894). The 3 mile section as far as the southern outskirts of Cwmbran is straightforward.

7 *The first time the canal ends, continue **SA** and you will soon rejoin it. The second time it ends (GR 293948) with a row of shops and the Halfway PH to the left, **turn L** then after 200 yds **turn R** onto Clomendy Road ('No through road except for bikes'). Descend to the roundabout, cross the road coming in from the left and continue in the same direction on the pavement alongside the dual carriageway. Soon rejoin the towpath.*

8 *You may follow the canal towpath for a further 3 miles although there is no sign nor any physical change in the towpath to indicate where the permitted section ends!*

19

INTO THE WOODED HILLS OF WENTWOOD FOREST SOUTH OF USK

DISTANCE
17 miles (27 kms)

TIME
3 hours

GRADE
Moderate

TERRAIN
River valley, arable land, forestry,
minor lane network

HILLS AND HIGHPOINTS
One major climb ▲ 750 ft (230 mts)
from the Usk valley to the turn off into
Wentwood Forest (Instruction 3)
Highest point ▲ 870 ft (265 mts)
in Wentwood Forest
Total ascent ▲ 1480 ft (450 mts)

START
The clocktower in the square, Usk
10 miles north of Newport, near the junction
of the A449 and the A472

PARKING
In and around the square

NEAREST RAILWAY
Newport, 7 miles southwest of the route at
Instruction 5

REFRESHMENTS
Lots of choice in Usk

*Usk is a charming market town
with a broad square and many
fine refreshment stops.
The town is set on the river of
the same name which rises
many miles to the west on the
slopes of the Black Mountain.
The ride explores the high
ground between the valleys
of the River Usk and the
River Wye, the other main
watercourse in southeast
Wales.*

Quiet lanes lead south from Usk for 5 miles, at first along the valley floor then very steeply into the wooded slopes of Wentwood Forest. The views through the edge of the forest back down into the Usk Valley are spectacular. Once out of the forest a series of tiny lanes and unclassified roads lead northwards through the hills and drop back down to the start in Usk

1 From the clocktower in the square in Usk take Priory Street 'Llantrisant 4'.

2 Follow this road for 5 miles, passing beneath the A449 dual carriageway. **Ignore** a right turn to Llantrisant. Climb to 750 feet, at times steeply.

3 At the top of the climb, shortly after passing a house on the left and just before a road turning to the left, **turn sharp R** onto a broad gravel track 'Bertholey House, Newbridge on Usk'. After ³/4 mile, at junction with better forestry track **bear L** (in effect SA).

4 After 1 mile, at fork of tracks with the Usk Valley Walk signposted to the right, **bear L** on the upper broad, forestry track. After ¹/2 mile follow the main track as it swings round 180 degrees.

5 After 1¹/2 miles at X-roads with minor lane go **SA, bearing slightly L**. At junction with better quality broad stone forestry track go **SA**.

6 At X-roads with 2nd lane go **SA** onto track past car park and follow track as it swings L away from car park / playground. At T-junction of forestry tracks **bear L**.

7 At X-roads of tracks at blue-ringed wooden marker go **SA**. At next X-roads of tracks after descent then short climb continue **SA** steeply uphill on narrow track. Climb up and over brow of the hill.

8 At X-roads with better track **SA**. At next X-roads, with views of a deep green valley ahead through the edge of the forest, **turn L** gently downhill. Follow the main track as it swings right in a wide arc. At T-junction with the road **turn L**.

9 After 1 mile take the **1st road R** by a triangle of grass. At next T-junction by larger triangle of grass and a newly-built house **turn R**.

10 After ³/4 mile take the **1st broad track L** 'White Horse Farm'. With the farm drive to the left **bear R** onto wooded track. At T-junction with tarmac **bear R**.

11 At fork of roads **bear L** towards house with slate roof. **Ignore** left turn by farm. At T-junction **turn L** downhill then shortly on sharp left hand bend at bottom of hill **bear R** (in effect SA) onto No Through Road.

12 Tarmac turns to track then the track narrows. Superb descent. **Bear L** at two T-junctions in quick succession.

13 At T-junction by white dotted line **bear L** (in effect SA). Go past a chapel on the right. At X-roads **turn R** 'Usk Flood Route'.

14 At T-junction by pub **turn L** to return to the start.

20

TWO LOOPS IN THE WYE VALLEY BETWEEN REDBROOK AND TINTERN

DISTANCE
One loop of 17 miles (27 kms)
One loop of 8 miles (13 kms)

TIME
4½ hours for both loops

GRADE
Moderate

TERRAIN
Steep wooded slopes, pasture and arable land, magnificent Wye Valley views

HILLS AND HIGHPOINTS
1st climb (1st loop) ▲ 820 ft (250 mts)
Brockweir to north of Cleddon
2nd climb (2nd loop) ▲ 590 ft (180 mts)
Redbrook to Wyegate Green Farm
Highest point ▲ 885 ft (270 mts)
north of Cleddon
Total ascent ▲ 1800 ft (550 mts)

START
Redbrook, 2 miles south of Monmouth on the A466

PARKING
In the car park opposite the church (used to be Little Chef). If you use the Boat Inn car park ask for permission from the pub, or go for a drink after the ride

NEAREST RAILWAY
Chepstow, 7 miles south of the route at Tintern

REFRESHMENTS
Boat Inn, Fish and Game PH, Redbrook
Brockweir Inn, Brockweir
Lots of choice in Tintern
Travellers Rest PH, Stowe
Ostrich PH, Newland

The first of two rides in the Wye Valley features a double dose of fun in the magnificent Wye Valley, two loops from the village of Redbrook to the south of Monmouth.

By making judicious use of the bridleway sections of the Offa's Dyke Path and the Wye Valley Walk plus a few forestry tracks it is possible to form loops from the valley floor up into the dazzlingly beautiful broadleaf woodlands that cloak the steep valley sides almost all the way from Chepstow to Monmouth. The ride starts easily enough alongside the Wye for several miles before climbing steeply on road up from Tintern into the forestry. A highpoint of almost 900 ft is reached to the north of Cleddon before a fast descent back down to the river at Redbrook. The second loop lies to the east of the river and uses the Coxbury and Wyegate Lane, now fallen into a fine state of disrepair, to climb up towards Newland with its excellent pub, descending back down to Redbrook along the course of an old coach road. Fine pubs, fine tracks, fine views and fine descents, what more could one ask for?

First Loop
(Redbrook-Brockweir-Redbrook).

1 Exit the car park opposite the church in Redbrook (the old Little Chef car park) at the left hand corner by the cypress trees. Then take the **second R** to cross the old railway bridge over the river. **Turn L by the Boat Inn, then L** again onto the course of the old railway. Follow for 2 1/2 miles.

2 At T-junction with the road **bear L** to continue in the same direction. At T-junction with the main road **turn L** to cross the river over Bigsweir Bridge. At the end of the bridge **turn R** onto Offa's Dyke Path, following the blue arrows/bridleway signs/horse signs for 3 1/2 miles over stone track, field edge and eventually alongside the river.

3 At the T-junction with the road in Brockweir, **either turn L** for the Brockweir Inn or **turn R to cross the river for continuation of the route.** At the T-junction with main road (A466) **turn L** for 3/4 mile towards Chepstow then just after the Wye Valley Hotel **turn R** 'Catbrook 2'.

4 Climb steeply for 2 miles.
At a T-junction at the top go **SA** onto forestry track 'Tintern, Whitestone' then after 20 yds **bear slightly L** up a steep, narrow, rough track. The track levels and passes through woodland.

5 At the road **turn L** past whitewashed, stone-built houses then after 1/2 mile, shortly after passing a house on the right called 'The Croft' **turn R** onto a track opposite a road turning on the left (this forms a sort of X-roads). Continue **SA** on the main track, ignoring tracks to right and left.

6 At the X-roads with a road go **SA** onto forestry track 'Maryland Forestry Commission'. **Easy to miss. Ignore** a major left turn then after 600 yards, at the end of a wide gravel car parking area to the right, **bear R** downhill on a narrow track.
At the T-junction with the road (by a red-brick bungalow) **turn L, then 1st road to the R**.

7 At the next T-junction **turn L then R** by the telephone box. Shortly after the forestry starts on the right **turn R** through a wooden barrier for a fast descent on broad forestry track.

8 At T-junction with dismantled railway path at the bottom of the hill **turn L** and rejoin the outward route, following the track back over the old railway bridge over the river back to the start.

Second Loop (Redbrook-Newland-
Redbrook via Coxbury and Wyegate Lane).

9 With back to the church in Redbrook **turn L** along the main road (A466) towards Chepstow.
200 yds after the Fish and Game PH, **turn L** sharply back on yourself onto Coach Road. After a further 200 yards take the **1st road to the R** steeply uphill 'Offa's Dyke Path'.

10 Tarmac turns to track on this steep climb. At a fork, with 'The Grove' signposted to the right, **bear L** onto the steeper, narrower stone track. The track continues climbing, widens then turns back to tarmac with superb views opening up.

11 *Shortly after the houses start follow the road around to the left. At T-junction* **turn L** *(The Travellers Rest PH is a short distance to the right). After* 1/2 *mile* **turn L on the first lane**.

12 *Tarmac turns to track at the farm and the track becomes grassy then narrow, steep and stony. At T-junction with the road* **turn L and then 1st L** *(For the Ostrich PH in Newland,* **do not** *take the second left but continue* **SA** *for 300 yards).*

13 **Main route.** *After* 1/2 *mile take the* **1st road to the L** *by a wooden shed and a stone-built bungalow 'Road Used as Public Path'. As the road swings left towards the water treatment works* **bear R** *(in effect SA) onto the broad stone track.*

14 *Go past a large stone farmhouse on the left and after a further 50 yds leave the main track and* **bear R** *downhill through a metal gate onto a broad grassy track. At a fork of tracks by a pond* **bear R** *and follow this track in the same direction as the track turns to tarmac. At T-junction with the main road (A466)* **turn sharply R** *to return to the start.*

21

THE WYE VALLEY FROM WYESHAM SOUTH OF MONMOUTH

DISTANCE
15 miles (24 kms)

TIME
3¹/2 hours

GRADE
Moderate

TERRAIN
Broadleaf woodland, sheep pasture,
the Wye Valley

HILLS AND HIGHPOINTS
1st climb ▲ 445 ft (135 mts)
up from Wyesham at the start
2nd climb ▲ 490 ft (150 mts)
from the Redbrook road up to Staunton
3rd climb ▲ 720 ft (220 mts)
from the Wye at Biblins Bridge to the
highpoint of the ride south of Staunton
4th climb ▲ 330 ft (100 mts)
from the Redbrook road back to Wyesham
Highpoint ▲ 790 ft (240 mts)
Total ascent ▲ 2750 ft (840 mts)

START
The church in Wyesham, southeast of
Monmouth. Take the A4136 towards Coleford
then first right onto Wyesham Road by the
Mayhill PH

PARKING
On the road past the church, schools
and shop in Wyesham

NEAREST RAILWAY
Lydney, 9 miles southeast near to Staunton

REFRESHMENTS
Mayhill Inn, Wyesham
White Horse Inn, Staunton
Ostrich Inn, Newland (just off the route)

*The second of two rides in
the Wye Valley, explores
the steep folds of broadleaf
woodland lying to the east of
Monmouth.
Starting in Wyesham the
route climbs on an atmospheric
sunken lane covered in green
ferns and bounded by moss-
covered drystone walls.
Once out of the woodland
the ride follows the course of
Offa's Dyke Path.*

Offa's Dyke Path is predominantly a footpath although there are bridleway or byway sections (such as the stretch used here) where it is possible to ride.
The route continues on road up to Staunton before dropping into the forest of Redding's Inclosure. Savour the best views of the day on the long descent down into the Wye Valley. Inevitably, a long climb follows the lovely riverside stretch. The A4136 is crossed, a final section of woodland is enjoyed before rejoining the outward route back to Wyesham.

1 With back to the church in Wyesham **turn R**. At the 'No through road' sign by a house called Springdale **turn L** uphill on narrow tarmac lane. Tarmac turns to track and climbs more steeply. Wonderful, dark, sunken green track past rock face and moss-covered drystone walls. Muddy in winter and after prolonged rain.

2 Emerge from woodland, reach brow of the hill by renovated stone cottage and join much better, broad stone track. Fast descent. At T-junction with the road **turn L** for 3/4 mile then **1st lane to the L** 'Staunton 1 1/4'. *(If this lane is closed, continue for 3/4 mile then on sharp right hand bend **bear L** then immediately left again).*

3 Climb steadily. At T-junction in Staunton **turn L** 'Monmouth'. At T-junction with the main road by the White Horse Inn **turn L** on A4136. **Easy to miss, after** 1/2 **mile turn sharply R** back on yourself onto forestry track. **Take care crossing this busy road.**

4 **Bear R at the 1st fork of tracks**. Fine, long descent. Go past a huge stone up to your right. At the next major fork **bear L** steeply downhill (good views). At the next junction at the bottom of the descent **turn R** to continue downhill. Follow the track parallel to the lovely River Wye. 400 yards after Biblins suspension bridge follow the main track as it swings right uphill away from the river.

5 Long steady climb. **Ignore** turnings to right and left, go **SA** at X-roads of tracks beneath power lines. At the first major

T-junction by a gravel clearing (with the left track climbing more steeply) **bear R** onto a slightly narrower track following the course of the brook. Shortly **turn R**.

6 Follow the main broad stone track gently uphill through broadleaf woodland. At T-junction with the main road **turn R then L**. After 1/4 mile take the **1st track R**. Go past a quarry on the left. At the T-junction **turn R**. **Ignore** the first right. At a T-junction with grassy tracks **turn R**.

7 At a T-junction with a minor lane **turn L**. After 1 1/2 miles at T-junction with more major road **turn R , then R again*** signposted 'Redbrook 1 1/2'.

* (Link to Ride 20. Turn **L** signposted 'Newland 1/2, Clearwell 2' past the Ostrich PH and take the **2nd road on the R** to join Ride 20 at Instruction 5).

8 **Easy to miss**, after 1 1/2 miles, shortly after houses, begin to keep an eye out for a tarmac drive on the right opposite a house called Woodlands on the left **turn R sharply back on yourself** 'Monmouth 3'. Climb steeply and follow the outward route back to the start.